A Safety Handbook for Science Teachers

The authors

K. Everett is Safety Officer at the University of Leeds. He was a member of the Safety Topic Group within the Science Teacher Education Project based on the universities of Reading and Leicester.

E. W. Jenkins is a Senior Lecturer in the Centre for Studies in Science Education, the University of Leeds. He was leader of the Safety Topic Group within the Science Teacher Education Project.

A Safety Handbook for Science Teachers

K. Everett

E. W. Jenkins

John Murray

First published 1973
Second edition 1977
Third edition 1980

Text set in 10/12 pt Linotron 202 Plantin, printed and bound
in Great Britain at The Pitman Press, Bath

0 7195 3760 6

Preface to the Third Edition

Since the first edition of this book appeared in 1973, there have been significant changes in the law relating to health and safety at work and a proliferation of the official and other advice offered to those responsible for teaching science in schools. In addition, a number of hazards of particular interest to science teachers have been identified and reported.

In the present edition, we have sought to reflect these developments as fully as possible while retaining an essential feature of a Handbook, that of offering advice and information in a compact but readily accessible form. Some matters, e.g. microbiological hazards, are treated in greater detail than in earlier editions and a number of new topics, e.g. dissection, the labelling of chemicals, have been included. The section dealing with the Classification of Fires has been revised completely and the bibliography and Appendix, reporting accidents in *The School Science Review* and *Education in Science*, have been brought up to date. There is a new Appendix offering detailed advice on procedure for human blood sampling and a new index has also been prepared.

The University of Leeds   K. Everett
Leeds   E. W. Jenkins
LS2 9JT

Acknowledgements

Particular acknowledgement is given to the University of Leeds for permission to quote extensively from the University of Leeds *Safety Handbook* and *Fire Precautions Handbook*.

We also wish to acknowledge the work of Mr S. C. Wilson who was largely responsible for compiling Appendix B; the contribution of Mr Hugh Perfect to discussions about the content of the chapter on Biological Hazards; the helpful advice and comment of colleagues and students within the University of Leeds, and the many useful suggestions which emerged during work on the Science Teacher Education Project.

We should also like to thank the University of Leeds for permission to reproduce illustrations on the following pages from the University publications shown: text illustrations on pp. 67, 69 (from *Safety Handbook*), pp. 51–58 (from *Fire Precautions Handbook*); marginal cartoons on pp. 2–4, 6, 9, 14, 26, 61 (from *Safety Handbook*), and the Association for Science Education Laboratory Safeguards Sub-committee for permission to reprint the advice, originally published in *Education in Science*, which appears as Appendix A.

The text illustrations listed above are the work of Miss Renee Bailey, Assistant Medical Illustrator within the Faculty of Medicine, the University of Leeds; others not listed are by Tony Mould but are based on illustrations in the University of Leeds publications. All the marginal cartoons are the work of John Wood.

Contents

1 Introduction

The prevention of accidents in laboratories is the duty of every individual using or entering them. For a teacher, ensuring the safety of others as well as of himself is of particular importance.

At the least, accidents result in wasted time, spoiled materials or broken apparatus. If there is also personal injury then pain and suffering are involved. Clearly it is the duty of every teacher to organize his classes in a way which reflects both his responsibility for their welfare and his commitment to teaching his pupils appropriate safety-conscious attitudes and behaviour.

Safety is to be regarded as a *positive factor* in science teaching and the teacher must therefore stress the importance of careful planning. Emphasis must be placed on adequate experimental design and on the acquisition of correct laboratory techniques. In this context two questions arise:

1 What is the most likely accident in a given situation?
2 What is the 'maximum credible' accident?

These imply an important third question:

3 How can accidents be prevented?

This book reflects the view that most accidents are better described as incidents which could have been prevented by adequate fore-thought. This in turn involves a recognition that pupils do not have the instinctive feeling for experimental work which a teacher will have acquired as a result of many years of experience. As a result what is commonsense to the teacher may well be totally outside the range of experience of a pupil and therefore be far from obvious to him.

One of the objects of adequate practical training in science, even at school, is to teach pupils how to handle safely materials which are potentially or actually dangerous.

Even so, every teacher should make it his or her task to become familiar with any special instructions issued for dealing with emergencies peculiar to the school in which he/she is working. Get to know the layout of the school—the location of fire-fighting equipment and how it works, ways of getting out of the building in an emergency, where telephones are sited and first aid arrangements. **Remember, it will be too late to find out very much when an emergency actually happens.**

If there is an accident your duties are as follows:

1 Assist any casualties.
2 Take appropriate steps to control the emergency.
3 Avoid becoming a casualty yourself.
4 Inform the appropriate authority (H.M., L.E.A.) that an accident has occurred. Many L.E.A.s have a standard form on which accidents should be recorded.

Action to be taken in an emergency

There are certain points which apply to all emergency situations:

1 Commit to memory the standing orders for action in an emergency. You will not have time to read them in an emergency.
2 You are expected to act in the spirit of the instructions. There is no substitute for informed common sense.
3 The most important consideration at ALL times is human safety.
4 Act quietly and methodically. This is likely to be the most effective way of retaining class control.
5 Ensure that pupils do not rush or attempt to pass others when leaving the scene of an accident.
6 As a teacher you must assume control of the situation, ensuring the safe evacuation from the premises of all pupils in your charge to an agreed assembly point. Be prepared to warn the Fire Brigade etc. of any known special hazards, e.g. gas cylinders, radioactive sources.
7 Remember that if you become a casualty someone must rescue you, possibly at personal risk to himself.
8 An accident to the teacher may be a major emergency. Contingency plans should take account of this possibility: (a) prevention by using safety screens etc.; (b) by instructing pupils what to do.

Use of telephone in an emergency

When telephoning for assistance in an emergency, give the following information:

(i) the location from which you are telephoning,
(ii) the type of emergency and the kind of assistance required,
(iii) the place where the assistance is required.

To ensure that the message has been correctly received, ask for it to be repeated to you.

Water emergencies, flooding

Attention is drawn to the very large variations in water mains pressure which occur at certain times of the day in large buildings. It is essential that pupils are taught to use screw clips or wire to secure condenser tubing. Water-cooled apparatus likely to be left unattended for any length of time must be fitted with an appropriate 'fail-safe' device to accommodate any failure in the water supply.

Every teacher must have ready access to the mains water tap in any laboratory in which he is teaching. This tap, along with other mains controls (gas, electricity, steam), should be located near the exit door from the laboratory. Note that a laboratory floor, made slippery by the spillage of a quite small quantity of water, constitutes a significant hazard.

2 Safety in laboratories and workshops

Apparatus not in immediate use should be put away, either in a store room or in a cupboard.

Do not place quantities of flammable or other dangerous materials near exits. In ground floor laboratories arrange the apparatus to allow access to emergency escape routes.

ALWAYS KEEP THE QUANTITIES AND VARIETY OF DANGEROUS MATERIALS TO A MINIMUM

Note that some Local Education Authorities specify the maximum quantities of individual substances which schools of various types may hold in stock.

Passages between benches and pieces of equipment should permit free circulation under normal working conditions. Obstruction of passages or interference with access to switches, fire extinguishers or other emergency equipment should not be permitted. Controls, switches, taps etc. should always be between the teacher and any apparatus he is using for demonstration purposes.

A correct height for a working surface is an underestimated factor in laboratory safety. For advice, see D.E.S. Building Bulletin No. 50, *Furniture and equipment, working heights and zones for practical activities*, H.M.S.O., 1973.

Guard against overhanging or jutting items. Lengths of metal or glass tubing should not be allowed to jut out into gangways.

The British Standards publication, BS 4163 (1975), *Recommendations for Safety in Workshops of Schools and Colleges of Education*, should be available in every school with workshop facilities. The following points are of particular importance:

1 During the demonstration of workshop techniques, great care must be taken to ensure that pupils do not lean over machines or tools in order to obtain a better view.

2 The importance of correct technique as a safe procedure should be emphasized.

3 The clearing away of waste or scrap materials should be demanded at all times.

Teachers should also consult Chapter 5 of *Safety in Further Education*, D.E.S. Safety Series, No. 5, H.M.S.O., 1976.

Offices, libraries and general areas

A recent nation-wide survey has revealed that offices are the scene of a substantial number of serious accidents every year. Most of these are avoidable. There is an increasing use of machinery in offices, e.g. paper-guillotines, duplicators etc., which should only be operated according to the makers' instructions. Only maintenance personnel should remove the enclosing panels of machines.

Portable electric fires and fans should be fitted with approved guards and leads should not be allowed to trail in a manner likely to cause persons to trip over them or pull the item over. Do not place them in precarious positions or where long hair can become ignited or entangled.

Do not use waste-paper baskets as ashtrays.

When carrying files, do not carry so many that your vision is obscured.

Filing cabinets should always have enough weight in the bottom drawers to prevent a full and open top drawer causing the cabinet to tip forward.

Filing cabinets of more than three drawers should, if possible, be anchored to the wall near the top of the cabinet.

Filing cabinet drawers should be closed as soon as you have found what you want, especially in crowded offices. The corner of a metal drawer can inflict a very painful injury.

NEVER stand on revolving stools or chairs and avoid using any chair or stool where steps are provided. A fall on to the end of a desk or an open drawer can cause a very serious injury.

Do not leave stacks of boxes or files on the floor near doorways for people to fall over.

The use of glass-ware

Glassware is produced and used in vast quantities and considerable variations in quality occur. Carboys and Winchester bottles should be treated with especial care. The wall thickness may occasionally be less than 1 mm. Many accidents have occurred through lifting full Winchesters by the neck, the weight of the contents being sufficient to shatter the bottle. NEVER pick up Winchesters by the neck.

Always ensure that carboys containing liquid are vented. If a full carboy is brought from a cool store into a warm room without being vented the slight rise in temperture can pressurize the carboy to bursting point. (The sudden appearance of 40 litres of concentrated acid on the laboratory floor is not amusing.)

NEVER store containers of liquids on the laboratory floor if there is underfloor heating. This is highly dangerous where volatile organic solvents are concerned.

It is bad practice to keep bottles of any chemicals, but especially liquids, in direct sunlight. Very sharp increases in temperature of the contents can take place. Beware of the burning glass effects of liquids in spherical glass containers. The sun shining through a flask of liquid placed on a window ledge can start a fire, the flask acting as a lens.

Great care should be taken when handling glassware and any broken glass should be cleared up AT ONCE. A PIECE OF PLASTICINE IS VERY USEFUL FOR COLLECTING SMALL SLIVERS OF GLASS. Put the broken bits in a cardboard box, a hessian sack or receptacle provided for broken glass. THE PERSON DISPOSING OF THE WASTE MAY GET CUT VERY BADLY THROUGH YOUR THOUGHTLESSNESS. Be particularly careful to ensure the removal of any broken glass from sinks. The use of chipped or cracked glassware should be avoided.

Always carry lengths of glass tubing vertically.

When breaking glass use a cloth or other suitable material to protect the hands.

When inserting glass tubing in bungs use the technique illustrated below. The procedure may, of course, be used in reverse for removing a seized tube from a bung.

All glassware should be thoroughly inspected for flaws. Any that are detected should either be repaired or the item rejected. Ensure that the correct type of glass is being used, e.g. boro-silicate, soda-glass etc.

A safe technique for threading glass tubing through rubber bungs, corks etc.

1 Select the appropriate sized stop-cock and bung.

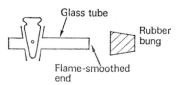

Glass tube

Rubber bung

Flame-smoothed end

2 Choose the correct size cork borer.

3 Lubricate the cork borer with e.g. glycerol, teepol, soft soap.

4 Bore the hole in the normal manner so that the operation leaves the borer in the bung with the hand-grip on the same side as that from which it is wished to insert the glass stop-cock.

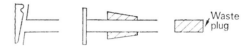

5 Select and lubricate the next largest cork borer and slide it over the first until it has passed through the bung.

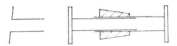

6 Withdraw the smaller cork borer and slide the glass tube into position.

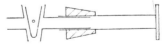

7 Withdraw the cork borer.

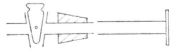

The use of pipettes

Mouth-operated pipettes are inexpensive to purchase. They are also dangerous if incorrectly used. The principal hazard when pipetting is failure to keep the tip of the pipette fully immersed in the liquid being sampled. Mouth-operated pipettes must NEVER be used for dispensing the following:

(i) volatile liquids, e.g. organic solvents, aqueous ammonia,
(ii) concentrated acids or caustic alkalis—caustic alkalis also attack glass and should not be used in accurately calibrated glassware,
(iii) toxic solutions or liquids,
(iv) radioactive materials.

Note also that the D.E.S. advises that there should be no mouth pipetting of any solution having a concentration greater than 0.1M.

Automatic pipettes and rubber pipette fillers are readily available from the usual commercial suppliers and their use in the laboratory should be encouraged. Pipettes should always be cleaned immediately after use and the practice of storing pipettes in a proper rack be emphasized. Laying a pipette on the laboratory bench can result in the mouthpiece becoming contaminated.

The use of burettes

When properly held in a clamp, the top of a burette is above the level of the user's head. The burette should be released and brought down below eye level before an attempt is made to fill it using a funnel. Pupils must not be allowed to climb on stools to fill burettes.

Cleaning glass-ware

Glass is not a completely inert material. It should always be cleaned as soon as possible after use.

Cleaning should commence with the mildest possible agent and every effort should be made to avoid the need to use such reagents as 'chromic acid'. Modern cleansing agents are safer and more effective. On no account should a chromic acid mixture be stored for occasional use in cleaning glassware.

Laboratory glassware must NEVER be used as drinking vessels.

Glassblowing

Gas supplies to glassblowing benches should be fitted with non-return valves which are approved by local Gas Board officials. This is particularly important if compressed air or oxygen is to be used.

Suitable glassblowing torches should be selected in accordance with the nature of the gas to be used, e.g. North Sea gas, coal gas, propane. These gases have different flame characteristics and practice in their use is essential.

Glassblowing benches should be fitted with extract ventilation to remove combustion products which may include toxic oxides of nitrogen when North Sea gas/oxygen flames are being used.

Laboratory sinks

Particular hazards are associated with the use of laboratory sinks made of polythene or polypropylene. Although such sinks have an excellent resistance to most acids, they may be distorted by organic solvents or even by dilute mineral acids at temperatures in excess of 70 °C. Most plastic sinks are flammable and easy to ignite and the advice of the safety committee of the A.S.E. is (i) that polythene or polypropylene sinks should not, in future, be fitted in laboratories, (ii) that, where such sinks have been fitted, suitable notices should be posted warning that they constitute a fire hazard if hot, burning or flammable materials are discarded in them.

For a summary of the relative merits of plastic, stainless steel and ceramic sinks see: *Education in Science*, 1975, 65, p. 32.

General chemical hazards

1 Solutions spilled on the bench or floor should be cleaned up immediately. Concentrated acids should be neutralized with an excess of solid sodium carbonate. Caustic alkali solutions should be treated with ammonium chloride and plenty of water. Protective clothing should be worn, especially eye-shields, during cleaning up.
2 Concentrated solutions should be diluted before they are poured down the sink and then washed away with large volumes of water to ensure that traps and settling pots are flushed thoroughly.
3 Do not point test tubes at other people.
4 Do not look into the mouth of a test tube or flask whilst you are mixing or heating the contents.
5 Do not sniff at possibly toxic materials.

At least one of the following guides to chemical hazards should be readily available in a school science department. C.L.E.A.P.S.E. *Hazcards,* 1978 (Available only to L.E.A.s which are members of the Consortium); Muir, G. D. (ed.), *Hazards in the Chemistry Laboratory*, Chemical Society, London, 1977; Scottish Schools Science Equipment Research Centre, *Hazardous Chemicals: A Manual for Schools and Colleges,* Oliver and Boyd, 1979.

Toxic substances and vapours

Toxic materials can enter the system via the lungs (inhalation), through open wounds, through the intact skin (absorption), or through the mouth (ingestion). Inhalation is a much greater hazard than ingestion. Because unhealed cuts present a direct entry to the blood stream for toxic agents they should always be covered by a waterproof plaster.

A useful guide to toxicity levels will be found in the publications by Muir and the S.S.S.E.R.C. (above). For a more comprehensive source of toxicity data, see Christensen, H. E. (ed.), *Register of Toxic Effects of Chemical Substances*, U.S. Department of Health, Education and Welfare, Washington D.C. Information may also be obtained from the office of the local Health and Safety Inspectorate and from the *Guidance Notes* on *Threshold Limit Values* issued by the Health and Safety Executive.

**Poisons, corro-
sives and irritants**

Many people working with chemicals, whilst sparing no effort to avoid cross-contamination of their reagents, often disregard the possibility of poisoning the person by contamination and too frequently long term hazards are overlooked, particularly where cumulative poisons are concerned. Major hazards exist with:

carbon monoxide, which is odourless;

hydrogen sulphide, which causes olfactory fatigue;

nitrous fumes, which may not produce symptoms until many hours after the exposure;

beryllium which, because of its extreme toxicity, is subject to statutory regulations;

benzene, which attacks the blood-forming organs;

mercury and lead, which are cumulative poisons;

tetrachloromethane, which attacks the liver and which oxidizes easily to phosgene (carbonyl chloride).

dimethylbenzenes (xylenes), which are absorbed chiefly through the lungs. The fate of the xylenes in the body has not yet been determined but inhalation causes headaches, fatigue and anorexia.

Note that the use of benzene in schools and other education establishments is the subject of a circular from the Department of Education and Science to L.E.A.s (M 72/0143, dated 2 April 1974). The advice given is that benzene should not be used at all as a solvent and that the use of benzene as a chemical reagent should be reduced to the absolute minimum.

Mercury must also be used with care. The element may be absorbed through the skin but inhalation of the vapour is a more common mode of entry into the body. Everyone concerned with handling mercury in a school should be made aware of the hazards of mercury vapour and appropriate warning notices should be displayed. Where possible, an alternative to mercury should be used. If mercury is being used, the hands must be protected and the procedure carried out under well-ventilated conditions. Mercury surfaces should not be exposed to the atmosphere for any length of time. Note that covering mercury with a layer of water does not prevent vaporization of the metal. If it is necessary to have a mercury surface exposed to the atmosphere, it should be covered with thin oil or sealed with paraffin wax. Mercury should not be heated in contact with an open atmosphere.

Experiments involving mercury should be done on a tray to facilitate recovery of any spillage. Mercury from broken thermometers should be recovered immediately by means of a capillary tube attached to a flask and filter pump. Mercury which cannot be recovered from crevices or cracks should be sprinkled with sulphur. It is sometimes convenient to treat spilt mercury with a mixture of solid carbon dioxide ('dry ice') and propanone and then sweep up the solid mercury.

It is not worthwhile purifying mercury in schools. A supplier will generally take back impure mercury with an excellent allowance against a new purchase. A film of dirt may be removed by shaking the mercury, gently, in a strong bottle containing a few pieces of sellotape.

For further advice see: *Mercury and Compounds of Mercury*, booklet no. 13 in the series *Methods for the Detection of Toxic Substances in Air*, H.M.S.O., *Mercury: Health and Safety Precautions*, Guidance Note EH17, Health and Safety Executive 1977 and 'Precautions in the Use of Mercury', *School Science Review*, 1978, 209, **59,** pp. 750–753.

Among the corrosive chemicals special note should be taken of hydrogen fluoride, either liquid or in aqueous solution. Any contamination with either should ALWAYS be treated as serious. Wash off with copious amounts of water and get medical treatment immediately. An injection is sometimes necessary and the medical officer should be forewarned of the possibility of an accident involving hydrogen fluoride. N.B. There is a delay of about 12 hours before the very painful effect of hydrogen fluoride contamination of the skin commences.

Do not overlook the fact that most organic solvents dissolve the protective secretions of the skin and that DERMATITIS, ALLERGIC reactions and even CARCINOMA can result from carelessness over a period of time depending upon the individual concerned.

Cancer hazards   Some aromatic amines and nitro-compounds are known to induce cancer in man some years after the initial exposure. Examples include 2-naphthylamine, benzidine, 4-aminodiphenyl, 4-nitrodiphenyl, and their salts. A number of other substances such as iodomethane (methyl iodide) and (chloromethyl)benzene (benzyl chloride) have been shown to induce cancer in laboratory animals. For carcinogenic plant material see page 49.

The relevance of chemical carcinogen hazards to school science teaching has been reviewed in *The School Science Review*, 1969, 175, **51,** p. 282 and in *Education in Science*, 1979, 84, pp. 17–20. Schools sometimes contain stocks of known carcinogens, particularly of some aromatic amines. Regulations forbid certain of these known carcinogens from being used or kept in schools. For details see:

> *Avoidance of carcinogenic aromatic amines in schools and other educational establishments*, D.E.S. Administrative Memorandum 3/70
>
> *Use of carcinogenic substances in educational establishments*, Scottish Education Dept. circular 825, 1972.

These two documents make similar points. The following substances should not be kept or used in schools:

1-and 2-naphthylamines
nitrosamines
nitrosophenols
nitronaphthalenes
some substituted diphenyls, e.g. benzidine (biphenyl-4,4'-diamine) *o*-dianisidine
chloroethene (vinyl chloride monomer)

Similar restrictions apply to the salts of these substances and to preparations in which they or their salts are likely to be present. Note that some aromatic amines, although relatively safe when pure, may present a hazard because they contain carcinogenic impurities. In general, a compound likely to contain, as an impurity, any of the substances referred to in the Memorandum or Circular cited above should not be used in schools. Among the substances with carcinogenic potential found in schools are dioxan, hydrazine, 8-hydroxyquinoline, ninhydrin, thioethanamide (thioacetamide), thiourea, trichloromethane (chloroform) and trichloroethene. Many of these substances are also toxic and volatile. Wherever possible, therefore, substitutes should be used. If this is not practicable, protective gloves and eye protection must be worn and precautions taken against the inhalation of vapour.

Although compounds of chromium and nickel have been reported widely to be carcinogenic, it is unlikely that most of the inorganic compounds of these elements pose significant carcinogenic hazards when used properly on a small scale in schools. However, compounds of chromium(VI) are a hazard to the skin and suitable precautions must be taken when using or producing these materials. The release into the general atmosphere of spray (e.g. from electrolysis) or dust (e.g. from thermal decomposition of ammonium dichromate(VI)) should be avoided.

The small scale distillation of crude oil should raise few carcinogenic hazards if conducted properly.

The possibility of generating a carcinogenic or suspected carcinogenic substance as a by-product of a routine laboratory reaction should not be overlooked. Methanal (formaldehyde) and hydrogen chloride react rapidly in air to form an appreciable concentration of bis-chloromethylether, a substance known to induce tumour-formation in rats exposed to an inhaled air concentration as low as 0.1 ppm. This substance is also formed in aqueous and non-aqueous media and in Friedel–Crafts' reactions using methanal and a variety of metal chlorides. Hence, the possibility of its formation must be considered whenever methanal and hydrochloric acid come into contact either by design or fortuitously (e.g. cleaning biological glassware).

Where concentrated hydrochloric acid is specified in preparations of condensation polymers involving methanal, it is usually possible to use 10 M (c. 50% aqueous) sulphuric acid instead. The A.S.E. advises that concentrated hydrochloric acid should not be stored in biology laboratories or preparation rooms nor methanal in chemistry laboratories or preparation rooms.

Asbestos

Inhalation of asbestos dust is known to lead to the possibility of a number of conditions, including fibrosis of the lung tissue (asbestosis), cancer of the lung and malignant tumours of the pleura and peritoneum (mesothelioma). The last condition is specially associated with blue asbestos and even low concentrations of this substance are to be regarded as constituting a major hazard. White asbestos also carries a carcinogenic risk, although it is unlikely that the concentration of white asbestos fibres in the atmosphere of a school science laboratory would reach a hazardous level.

A range of products is available to replace asbestos items in laboratories. In schools, therefore, asbestos and asbestos products should not be used. Asbestos mats and tape may be replaced by products made of ceramic materials and stainless steel, or ceramic-centred, iron-wire tripod gauzes may be used instead of the more common asbestos-centred variety. Ceramic fibre wool or a mineral wool such as Rocksil should be used as an alternative to asbestos wool. Note, however, that Rocksil is made from blast furnace slag and has, therefore, a variable composition. In particular, it may contain oxidizable impurities and minor explosions have been reported on heating the mineral wool with a strong oxidizing agent such as potassium manganate(VII). Portions of a new stock of Rocksil should, therefore, be roasted strongly before use in this way. Ceramic fibre wool is resistant to most chemicals but is attacked by concentrated alkalis. It is available in a platinized form for use as a catalyst. For most school purposes thick, heat resisting, leather gloves provide an adequate alternative to gloves made of asbestos.

The use of asbestos in schools is governed by the D.E.S., Administrative Memorandum 7/76, *The Use of Asbestos in Educational Establishments*, and S.E.D. Circular 668, 1968.

Handling, storage and transport of chemicals

Many chemicals are poisonous, corrosive or otherwise objectionable. Many people who enter laboratories, e.g. caretakers, cleaners, pupils, have an inadequate training to appreciate this fully. For your own safety and that of others, ensure that all corrosive or poisonous materials are stored under safe conditions and properly labelled.

Prime emphasis must be placed on preventing chemicals in any form coming into contact with extraneous matter. Neatness and cleanliness in the laboratory are essential. If acid or strong alkali is spilt, the cleaning-up should be carried out immediately under experienced supervision and care taken when disposing of the waste, e.g. never mop up concentrated nitric acid or other oxidizing acids with a dry cloth or sprinkle sawdust on them.

Experiments with dangerous chemicals should be carried out behind safety screens, i.e. GUARD AT SOURCE. If obnoxious fumes will be evolved, use a fume-cupboard.

Provision should be made for containing chemicals in the event of a breakage or spillage, e.g. apparatus containing mercury should be placed in a tray (from the point of view of both health and economy).

Always exercise care when opening laboratory doors.

EXCEPT IN THE MOST DIRE EMERGENCY NO ONE SHOULD EVER RUN IN A LABORATORY OR ALONG CORRIDORS JOINING LABORATORIES

Do not place corrosive chemicals on shelves above the shoulder of the smallest person in the laboratory.

School science laboratories are not suitable places in which to store chemicals in stock quantities and separate storage facilities should be an integral part of the provision made for the teaching of practical science. If a storage area is also to be used as a preparation room, it must be sufficiently large and so located that equipment and chemicals can be carried safely and easily into the laboratories, preferably by means of trolleys of the same height as the laboratory benches. Stock quantities of common, volatile liquids such as carbon disulphide, ethanol, propanone (acetone) and methylbenzene (toluene) must be stored in a specially constructed store outside the laboratory. For details of the design of an outside store, see Everett,

K., Hughes, D., *A Guide to Laboratory Design*, Butterworths, 1975. No more than 500 cm³ of any one volatile, flammable liquid should be kept in bottles on laboratory benches or shelves and all such bottles must be clearly labelled 'Highly Flammable'.

Give particular attention to the storage and use of reagents which are known to deteriorate with time. New stock should be date stamped on receipt and substances ordered in amounts which permit a steady turn-over and prevent the accumulation of old stock. Diethyl ether (ethoxyethane) sometimes contains explosively unstable peroxides after prolonged storage and the formation of such substances in alcohols or alcohol mixtures under similar conditions has also been reported. Any peroxide may be detected by the liberation of iodine on the addition of acidified, aqueous potassium iodide to the suspect alcohol or ether. Testing for peroxide formation should be a routine procedure before distilling any alcohol or ether which has been stored for any length of time. Re-distilled ether should be stored in a cool place in a dark bottle containing a small coil of clean copper wire. Note that some fluids used in wet copying processes contain a very high proportion of an alcohol such as propan-2-ol.

The storage of alkali metals also needs special attention. Potassium has been known to corrode the aluminium cans in which it is usually stored in schools.

For an introduction to some aspects of laboratory stock control, see Archenhold, W. F., Jenkins, E. W., Wood-Robinson, C., *School Science Laboratories, A handbook of design, management and organization*, Murray, 1978.

The Labelling of Chemicals

The Packaging and Labelling of Dangerous Substances Regulations, 1978, issued as Statutory Instrument No. 209, 1978, came fully into operation on 1 March 1979 and require suppliers to label, in a specified manner, containers used for the handling or storage of the substances prescribed by the Regulations. The particulars to be shown on a label include a maximum of two of the following hazard warning symbols. Radioactive materials are governed by other regulations.

Harmful substances | Corrosive substances | Explosive substances | Oxidizing substances | Flammable substances | Toxic substances

Teachers, technicians, pupils and all others with a legitimate access to a laboratory should be familiar with these symbols and the significance to be attached to each of them.

Note, however, that:

1 The Regulations apply to suppliers only and not to users.
2 The Regulations do not apply to 'preparations' even though these may present hazards e.g. Millon's reagent.
3 The Regulations were not devised with schools particularly in mind. As such, some of the advice given in Schedule 4 of the Regulations may be inappropriate e.g. 'Keep locked up and out of the reach of children'.
4 Where a substance is not explosive, toxic or corrosive, and/or the container is of '125 millilitres capacity or less', some of the requirements are relaxed.
5 Suppliers are sometimes required to display different symbols or advice on containers of solutions of different concentrations.

It follows, therefore, that THE ABSENCE OF A HAZARD SYMBOL OR STATEMENT FROM THE LABEL OF A CONTAINER DOES NOT NECESSARILY MEAN THAT THERE ARE NO HAZARDS ASSOCIATED WITH ITS CONTENTS.

In these circumstances, a school science department should adopt a sensible labelling policy designed to minimize any inconsistencies. Hazard symbols may be purchased from the usual laboratory suppliers as gummed labels or as tape. For further advice, see *Education in Science*, 1979, 82, pp. 25–26.

Violent reactions

The following list, by no means exhaustive, indicates a number of hazardous materials or mixtures which can react suddenly and violently with little or no warning:

(a) strong or concentrated acids with strong or concentrated bases;
(b) oxidizing agents with (i) metal powders, (ii) reducing agents;
(c) alkali metals and/or alkali earth metals with water, acids or chlorinated solvents; consequently, neither sodium nor potassium may be used for drying such solvents as trichloromethane (chloroform) or tetrachloromethane (carbon tetrachloride); note that explosions have occurred when small pieces of lithium have been heated in air, particularly in conditions of high humidity;

(d) metal hydrides;

(e) hydrocarbons with halogens, chromic acid or sodium peroxide;

(f) concentrated nitric acid–alcohol mixture (reacts only after a latent period);

(g) liquid bromine.

A list of accidents reported in *The School Science Review* over the period 1919–79, and in *Education in Science* is included in Appendix B (p. 88).

For a comprehensive, indexed guide to published data, see Bretherick, L., *Handbook of Reactive Chemical Hazards*, Butterworths, 1979.

Solid peroxides and concentrated solutions

If peroxides enter the eyes the probability of severe damage is so great that EYE PROTECTION MUST BE WORN WHEN HANDLING OR USING THESE SUBSTANCES.

Strict cleanliness of equipment should be observed, great care being taken to avoid contamination by other peroxides or incompatible materials. Do NOT return unused peroxides to the stock bottle. Peroxides should not be allowed to accumulate in store cupboards merely because a future use may arise. They should not be kept in direct sunlight or near heat sources, e.g. steampipes, fires, radiators. In polymerization experiments, di(benzoyl) peroxide, (benzoyl peroxide) should be replaced by di(dodecanoyl) peroxide, (lauroyl peroxide) which is much less hazardous to store and handle.

Most peroxides are decomposed by caustic soda, e.g. di(benzoyl) peroxide may be disposed of by adding it carefully, a little at a time, to ten times its own weight of 10% aqueous sodium hydroxide. The reverse procedure should NOT be undertaken.

For further advice on the storage of organic peroxides see:
Code of Practice for the Storage of Organic Peroxides, Laporte Chemicals Ltd, P.O. Box 7, Warrington, Lancashire.

Plastics and polymers

The number of plastic and polymeric materials available to, and used in, schools has grown rapidly in recent years. The following points should be noted:

1 Only small quantities of plastic materials should be heated for test purposes. Polystyrene produces toxic styrene vapour on heating

and PVC yields hydrogen chloride. Strong heating of acetal resins leads to the evolution of methanal and acrylic materials decompose to give methyl methacrylate (2-methylpropenoate)

2 Expanded polystyrene should be cut by a hot wire which is not sufficiently hot to cause the liberation of the toxic monomer. Expanded polystyrene should not be sanded or sawn except under conditions where the dust can be prevented from entering the lungs.

3 Protective gloves must be worn whenever hot plastics, resins or adhesives are handled in the laboratory.

4 Where polymerization reactions are catalysed by peroxides, di(dodecanoyl) peroxide, (lauroyl peroxide) should be used in preference to di(benzoyl) peroxide, (benzoyl peroxide).

5 A number of organic reagents (trichloromethane, 1,2-dichloroethane, glacial ethanoic (*acetic*) acid) are commonly used to bond acrylic materials. The hazards associated with these materials are well known and appropriate precautions should be observed. Note that solutions of acrylic materials in ethanoic acid can cause severe and delayed blistering of the skin.

6 Friction welding of acrylic materials should not be undertaken in school science workshops or laboratories.

7 Poly(tetrafluoroethene), P.T.F.E., should not be overheated as this may lead to the influenza-like symptoms of 'polymer-fume fever'.

8 Methyl ethyl ketone peroxide, M.E.K.P., is often used in conjunction with an accelerator of cobalt naphthenate to catalyse the setting of resins. M.E.K.P. and cobalt naphthenate together constitute an explosive mixture. Hence, it is advisable to use resins which incorporate the accelerator and require only the addition of the M.E.K.P. catalyst.

9 The D.E.S. advises that polyurethanes should not be prepared in schools. On no account should polyvinyls be synthesized in a school laboratory.

Cracking reactions

A number of school texts suggest a procedure for converting naphtha into a fuel gas by means of a cracking reaction. In some instances, the catalyst suggested is pyrophoric in nature and, in any event, the procedure is hazardous unless all air is removed from the apparatus.

Waste disposal

Much of the legislation governing waste disposal, water pollution, atmospheric pollution and noise has been incorporated in the Control of Pollution Act 1974.

Under this Act, a Disposal Authority (a county council in England) has wide responsibility for providing adequate arrangements for the disposal of 'controlled waste' (i.e. commercial, industrial, household or any such waste) and for preparing a plan for all aspects of waste disposal. Depositors of waste must be licensed by a Disposal Authority which may impose conditions for disposal in granting the licence. There are severe penalties for contravention of the provisions of the Act.

In schools, the quantities of toxic, noxious or otherwise hazardous material which must be destroyed are usually small. Where possible, therefore, such materials may be rendered harmless by the science teacher by incineration, dilution or chemical treatment as appropriate. Where materials cannot be disposed of easily and safely by one of these methods, appropriate arrangements must be made by a local education authority. The disposal of radioactive, carcinogenic or highly toxic materials raises special problems and the advice of the appropriate Disposal Authority must be sought unless the teacher is certain that he can dispose of such materials safely and legally. For a summary of the legal provisions relating to the disposal of radioactive waste, see Administrative Memorandum, 2/76, and the associated notes for guidance.

Local fire brigades will sometimes agree to collect and destroy flammable waste solvents. Any large teaching institution, e.g. a university, produces large quantities of such waste and will have made provision for its regular collection and disposal. It is sometimes possible for a nearby school to gain the cooperation of such an institution in disposing of flammable solvents.

School science accommodation must include provision for the safe collection of several different types of solid waste. Broken glass or porcelain must be kept in a clearly marked container, reserved for the purpose. Bacteriological or fungal cultures should be collected in a special container if the unwanted cultures cannot be destroyed immediately by autoclaving or rigorous chemical sterilization. Reactive chemicals, especially powerful oxidizing agents, must not be placed in waste bins. In general, stocks of hazardous materials such as potassium or white phosphorus should be kept at the minimum necessary to ensure adequate supplies for routine teaching purposes and experiments should be designed so that as little toxic material as possible is used or produced.

For a review of the problems of waste disposal in the light of the Health and Safety etc. Act 1974 and other relevant Acts see: Cook, J. D., Disposal of Toxic and Hazardous Chemicals, *Education in Chemistry*, 1975, 6, **12,** pp. 182–184.

Gas cylinders

Hazards associated with gas cylinders are of two types: (i) the physical hazards associated with the structure of the cylinders themselves, (ii) hazards associated with their contents.

Gas cylinders vary in size from the small canisters of fuel for camping stoves to the industrial or commercial sort. The very high pressure gas cylinders may have round or flat ends and the temptation to store the latter vertically without support must be resisted. Gas cylinders must ALWAYS be clamped in position or laid horizontally on the floor and WEDGED to prevent them rolling.

The weight of a gas cylinder may give a misleading impression of its strength. The 'weak' point of an industrial gas cylinder is the base of the valve stem and great care must be taken to ensure that the valve does not forcibly strike a hard surface. If the valve is in some way sheared off, e.g. by dropping or knocking over a cylinder, the cylinder becomes a jet-propelled missile. Particular care is needed when taking cylinders up or down stairs or steps.

Before use, the valve of every cylinder should be inspected and checked. Any loose dirt should be blown out of the seating before fitting the regulator. It is most important that the valve can be opened smoothly.

Do not allow familiarity with gas cylinders to breed contempt and so permit unwarranted liberties with them, especially with regard to the regulating valves. Most accidents with gas cylinders are due to maltreatment.

Stiff valves should be treated cautiously. It should be possible to open the valve by hand pressure using the standard key. DO NOT USE HAMMERS OR EXCESSIVE LEVERAGE, e.g. a Stilson wrench. Cylinders with stiff valves should be made safe and returned unused to the supplier with an explanatory note.

A GENTLE tap with a piece of wood is permissible on the wing nut which screws the pressure regulator into the cylinder head. Cylinder valves should always be tested in the open or in a well-ventilated area before being taken into a laboratory. Always blow foreign matter from the outlet before putting on the regulator valve.

Cylinders, valves, pressure reducers, gauges etc. for combustible gases have outlets and fittings screwed with a left-hand thread. Those for non-combustible gases are screwed with a right-hand thread.

ALL CONNECTIONS SHOULD BE MADE SECURE BY THE USE OF SUCH ITEMS AS 'JUBILEE' CLIPS.

Never empty a cylinder completely, but leave it with a slight positive pressure (say, 2 atmospheres*) and the valve closed to

* 1 atm $\cong$ 14 lb/in^2 $\cong$ 101 kPa.

prevent diffusion of air into the cylinder. This is especially important with flammable gases. When a cylinder is empty mark it clearly and unambiguously.

In all installations the cylinder key should be made captive to the cylinder to facilitate rapid cut-off in an emergency.

Explosions have been caused by the too rapid opening of the valve resulting in compression heating in the regulator. Oxygen cylinders are prone to this type of accident. NEVER USE GREASE OR OIL ON OXYGEN CYLINDERS OR LINES—they cause explosions.

Types of cylinder gases:

(a) *'Permanent' gases*, e.g. oxygen, nitrogen, carbon monoxide.
(b) *Liquefied gases*, e.g. carbon dioxide, sulphur dioxide, chlorine, nitrous oxide (dinitrogen oxide).
(c) *Dissolved gases*. The only example likely to be encountered is acetylene dissolved in acetone.

Identification of gas cylinders

The only legally recognized means of identifying a gas cylinder is the WRITTEN WORD—colours are merely a secondary guide. Cylinders of gas for medical use are painted differently from those for industrial use. Where American cylinders are in use especial care is needed as the U.S.A. colour code is completely different from the British.

Acetylene (Ethyne)

Only approved regulating valves may be used and no pipe fitting of copper or alloy of copper containing more than 70% copper may be used for dry acetylene, to avoid the danger of moist acetylides forming.

With moist acetylene, explosive corrosion products can result where even low copper alloys are used and traces of mineral acid enhance the formation of explosive acetylides. The pressure in any piped acetylene system must never exceed 9 lb/in²★ above atmospheric pressure. The system must be fitted with a flame arrester and, if other gases are involved, non-return valves must be used.

The explosive limits for acetylene are:

in air   2–82%
in oxygen   2–93%

N.B. A heavy blow on an acetylene cylinder can ignite the contents as a result of adiabatic compression.

★ 9 lb/in² ≡ 62.05 kN m⁻².

Hydrogen

The combustion limits are:

in air   4–75%
in oxygen   4–94%

N.B. Too rapid opening of a valve can cause ignition due to static electricity.

Hydrogen is involved in a large proportion of school laboratory accidents. When lighting a jet of hydrogen, a sample must always be selected and tested to see that it is free from air *before* the jet is ignited. A similar testing procedure is necessary when town gas, rather than hydrogen, is used to reduce a metallic oxide. Where natural gas is supplied to laboratories, it may be necessary to use a hydrogen cylinder although some schools have adopted the practice of bubbling the natural gas through methanol or ethanol to increase the reducing property of the gas flow. In these circumstances, it is essential that all air is removed from an apparatus before attempting to ignite the gas mixture.

For a summary of safeguards in the laboratory preparation of hydrogen, see *Education in Science*, 1974, 60, p. 33.

Hydrogen sulphide

Hydrogen sulphide is an extremely toxic gas. 0.77 ppm has a faint but readily perceptible odour. The maximum permissible concentration is 20 ppm. 100 ppm paralyses the olfactory nerve so the gas can no longer be smelled. 700–900 ppm rapidly produces unconsciousness. 5000 ppm produces immediate unconsciousness due to paralysis of the respiratory centre.

Work on plants handling tonnage quantities has shown that alcohol in the system (consumed in the previous 16–24 hours) increases the susceptibility to hydrogen sulphide.

A person with a perforated eardrum should not work in areas of potentially toxic concentrations of hydrogen sulphide. Ear plugs do not give effective protection.

Oxygen

More than half the accidents due to compressed gases are caused by oxygen. Oxygen-enriched atmospheres increase the fire risk enormously, e.g. if the oxygen content of the atmosphere is increased from 21% to 24% clothing burns rapidly instead of smouldering.

Propane

The explosive limits of this gas, which is denser than air, are:

in air   2–10%
in oxygen   2–93%

Cylinders of LIQUEFIED OR DISSOLVED GASES MUST be used in a vertical position in an approved stand or chained or clamped to the wall or bench. It is also good practice to use cylinders of 'permanent' gases in a vertical holder—they take up less floor space and the valves are less likely to be kicked.

With 'permanent' gases, the pressure indicates the quantity of gas remaining in the cylinder but with liquefied or dissolved gases the enormous variation of pressure with temperature makes weighing the best guide. The withdrawal of dissolved gases, e.g. acetylene, at more than 20% of the cylinder content per hour entails the risk of contamination of the gas with solvent vapour.

Aerosols

Some laboratory reagents are now available in aerosol form, e.g. ninhydrin. Many of the substances used in aerosols are potentially hazardous. To prevent inhalation or skin absorption of these substances, aerosols should be used only in a fume cupboard or an alternative procedure, e.g. 'dipping', adopted. Aerosols should be stored in a cool place and any detailed instructions accompanying an aerosol be scrupulously observed.

Compressed air

Compressed air supplies in workshops and laboratories should be treated with respect—compressed air jets when misused can cause serious injuries. Compressed air can kill as swiftly as electricity. Cleaning swarf or dust from a machine should not be done with the compressed air line—use a brush or vacuum cleaner. A jet of compressed air playing on the body can introduce air into the bloodstream, especially if there are small scratches or punctures of the skin. Do not dry solvents from the skin with compressed air; both air and solvent can enter the bloodstream. Compressed air supplies to which students have access should carry a warning such as the one overleaf.

WARNING

Never direct a jet of compressed air against another person (**or yourself**).

Practical jokes with compressed air have caused horrifying injuries and death.

Vacuum systems

Much vacuum apparatus is constructed of glass, although more equipment made of plastics is now available, including vacuum desiccators. Glass vacuum desiccators should conform with the specifications of BS 3423, *Recommendations for the design of glass vacuum desiccators*.

When assembling vacuum apparatus examine the equipment for stresses and strains, both before and after filling the equipment. A kilogram of reagents (approximately 75 cm^3 mercury) can introduce severe strains in a glass apparatus. Use metal or plastic (PVC) tubing wherever possible and include flexible items in the apparatus, e.g. bellows couplings. When using ground glass unions, ball and socket joints are preferred to cone and socket joints.

If a piece of glassware is placed between two crossed polaroid sheets in front of a lamp, areas of strain in the glass will appear darker than the rest, indicating that further annealing is necessary.

As far as possible, vacuum apparatus should be screened. Wide bore tubing, bulbs and items up to about one litre capacity should be strapped with cloth, adhesive tape or cellophane tape, be covered with cloth mesh and varnished (or sprayed) with PVC. Larger items should be encased in a stout gauge wire screen. Safety goggles must be used when operating with glass vacuum apparatus.

ALWAYS ensure that rubber bungs are large enough to resist being sucked into a vacuum vessel.

Ensure that stop-cocks are properly lubricated and never try to force one.

Always operate stop-cocks SLOWLY.

Cryogenics

Extreme cold is the principal hazard involved in the use of cryogenic systems and liquefied gases, e.g. solid CO_2, liquid air. Prolonged contact with the skin may cause burns similar to those resulting from contact with extreme heat. Eye protection should be worn when handling these materials. A pad used as a pot holder is preferable to gloves.

Mechanical hazards

The principal hazards include injuries caused by moving parts, failure of equipment, incorrect or careless use of hand tools, faulty or damaged tools etc. Many accidents in this category can be avoided merely by the correct use of equipment that is well maintained and inspected.

All machines, whether hand- or power-operated should be fitted with appropriate guards or other safety devices. These should always be used. Correct protective clothing and other apparel appropriate to the work should be worn. Long hair should be protected by suitably fitting head-gear, e.g. hair-nets.

Centrifuges can very easily be damaged and are a source of danger when improperly used.

DO NOT try to stop a centrifuge with the hand. The periphery of a 10 cm radius rotor at 5000 rpm is travelling at over 180 km h^{-1} (110 mph).

ALWAYS balance the load on the centrifuge accurately before switching on to avoid putting undue stress on the bearings.

Keep the centrifuge clean. Corrosion can seriously weaken the rotor.

Laboratory centrifuges should comply with BS 4402 (1969) and should be used only in a manner prescribed or approved by the manufacturer. For servicing purposes, a record should be kept of the amount of use a machine receives. Heads and accessories should be inspected regularly for signs of cracks or corrosion and on no account should the specified maximum load for the centrifuge be exceeded.

Guillotines

All guillotines should be fitted with an appropriate guard.

Protective clothing

Appropriate protective clothing should be worn in laboratories and workshops by both pupils and teachers. To wear protective clothing is to recognize that a hazard exists. It is NOT an excuse for careless work. Dirty overalls or coats should not be tolerated, being in themselves a source of hazard.

Laboratory coats should be worn buttoned up. When unbuttoned and billowing about the wearer they are not only useless but a danger. These and similar items of clothing should not be allowed to hang freely, but be secured to prevent them trailing loosely over apparatus or machinery. Care should be taken in the choice of

materials. Most synthetic fibres are not absorbent and, in some circumstances, compare unfavourably with cotton as a protective medium. Also a substantial static charge can accumulate on a synthetic fibre garment.

Insufficient use is made in schools of eyeshields and protective spectacles. Effective and inexpensive plastic spectacles are readily obtainable for use by both teacher and pupils. Where necessary, such spectacles may be sterilized by washing with diluted Dettol or by enclosure in a plastic bag which is then filled with sulphur dioxide. Attention is drawn to the advice of the A.S.E. that 'protective spectacles be worn at all times when conducting experiments' and to that of the D.E.S. that 'whenever any operation with chemicals is performed, goggles must be worn'.

For a discussion of the use and storage of safety spectacles in the school laboratory see *School Science Review* 1973, 190, 55, pp. 190–191, which also lists some suppliers. Attention is also drawn to the *Protection of Eyes Regulations (1974)* (which came into force on 10 April 1975), to the relevant British Standards specifications for eye protectors, BS 1542 (1960) and BS 2092 (1967) and to paragraph 52 of *Safety in Science Laboratories*, H.M.S.O., 1978.

Safety screens, goggles or other eye protection must be used when glass apparatus is to be used under pressure as there is danger of splashing by solutions of strong chemicals.

White coats are neither status symbols nor magic talismen. Leave them and the contamination in the laboratory. DO NOT carry the contamination to tea rooms, libraries etc.: other people do not wish to share the odours and risks of your work.

Electrical hazards

Two of the worst electrical hazards are careless or unskilled workmanship and faulty or worn-out equipment. Neither of these hazards needs arise.

Plugs should be wired as follows:

1 Trim the wires and insulation to the correct length.

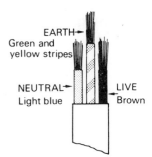

2 Twist the bare ends of the wire into a clockwise loop.

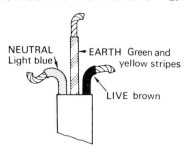

3 Wrap the trimmed wires round the appropriate terminals and screw down firmly.
Check that the wires are firmly gripped.

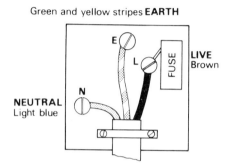

4 Fix the flex firmly by the strap so that no strain can be placed on the terminals in the plug.
5 Make sure that there are no loose strands of wire to cause short-circuits within the plug.
6 Replace the plug top.

Prior to July 1970, Continental and American wiring colour codes were different from British practice.

As from 1 July 1970, Great Britain and 18 other European countries have agreed to use a new colour code, as follows:

Earth	green and yellow	(stripes)
Live	brown	(dark)
Neutral	blue	(light)

This code has the advantage of being distinguishable by persons who are red/green colour blind.

Electric and electronic supplies and equipment, including batteries and electrolytic condensers, can be responsible for personal injury and even death, also for fires and explosions.

Do not smoke when using or examining lead/acid batteries. Hot tobacco ash can ignite the hydrogen/oxygen mixture produced during charging, and cause an explosion capable of shattering the battery case and throwing sulphuric acid (density 1.25 g cm⁻³) several feet.

Static electricity can cause fires and explosions, especially when pouring non-conducting flammable materials.

It is dangerous to service or modify equipment which is not completely disconnected from the mains.

DO NOT FORGET THAT CAPACITORS CAN DELIVER A POWERFUL SHOCK EVEN WHEN THE POWER SUPPLY IS ISOLATED. ALWAYS SHORT THE TERMINALS ON A CAPACITOR BEFORE ATTEMPTING TO SERVICE AN ITEM OF EQUIPMENT. (See p. 29 and the section on lasers, p. 33.)

Cables and leads should be of suitably covered material and adequately protected in atmospheres where corrosive chemicals or solvents are used. It is advisable to avoid using cotton-covered twin flexible cord in experimental circuits.

Adequate earths and suitable fuses should be used. Do not rely on simple soldered joints for an earth connection but use a screw as well: the soldered joint may be dry.

Cables should not be allowed to trail loosely across the floor or hang festooned like Christmas decorations but should be strapped into neat bundles and secured.

ALL NEW EQUIPMENT SHOULD BE CHECKED BEFORE USE TO ESTABLISH THAT THE CHASSIS IS NOT LIVE DUE TO A MANUFACTURING FAULT OR INCORRECT MAINS CONNECTION

High voltages

High voltages in conjunction with vacuum or gas discharge when the potential difference is 5 kV or more can produce biologically damaging radiations. The use of high voltages in vacuum or discharge tubes which may generate X-rays is therefore governed by the D.E.S. Administrative Memorandum 2/76 and the associated notes for guidance.

Electric shock

The smallest current which can be detected through the skin ('threshold of perception') is generally considered to be approximately 1 mA r.m.s. at 50 Hz a.c. and 5 mA d.c. (The tongue is considerably more sensitive.) On increasing the current a stage is reached at which severe muscular contractions make it difficult for the casualty to release his hold. This 'threshold of muscular decontrol' is about 15 mA at 50 Hz a.c. and 70 mA d.c.; in the lower frequency ranges the effect increases with frequency, e.g at 60 Hz the threshold current is 7 mA. Very high frequencies do not produce this effect. Increase in current beyond about 20 mA 50 Hz a.c. or 80 mA d.c. brings danger to life. The next stage is irregular contractions of the heart, leading to cessation of the pumping action.

This occurs at about 100 mA for both a.c. and d.c. and is almost certain to be fatal. If the current through the body rises as high as 1 A, severe burning results. The electrical resistance of the body can vary enormously from person to person and in the same person at different times and under different conditions. This resistance can be as high as 10 000 ohms or as low as a few hundred, depending largely on whether the skin is dry or moist. Even with a resistance of 10 000 ohms the 230 V a.c. supply will result in a current of more than 20 mA, which could be lethal.

In fact, much lower voltages can be dangerous and death has been recorded from only 60 V.

It will be appreciated that the above remarks apply essentially to current passing through the body, e.g. from hand to hand, or hand to foot. It is possible for part of the body, e.g. a finger, to short-circuit two conductors of differing potential or a charged capacitor. This will not necessarily result in electric shock as described above but it can inflict severe burns which will require medical treatment.

Capacitors

All high-grade capacitors and, in particular, large energy storage capacitors as used in pulsed capacitor banks, will recover a considerable proportion of the original charging energy if left on open circuit after discharge. This phenomenon is known as the 'residual effect', 'dielectric hysteresis' or 'dielectric absorption' effect and a capacitor is said to have an 'absorptive capacity'.

Experience has shown that recovery may be as much as 10% of the original voltage, and a 30 kV capacitor may build up to 2 or 3 kV in 10 minutes. Further, dangerous voltages can build up on open-circuited high voltage capacitors over a period of many months after discharge.

It has been found that a discharge of energy exceeding 10 joules into the human body can be hazardous to life, while 0.25 joule gives a heavy shock. Ten joules would be obtained by complete discharge of a capacitor charged as in the following table:

CAPACITY (μF)	0.002	0.2	20	80	320	2 000
CHARGED TO (kV)	100	10	1	0.5	0.25	0.1

It is essential that each spare or disconnected capacitor should be kept individually short-circuited by a robust connection when not in use.

It should also be remembered that 'new' capacitors have already been energized for test purposes, and should also be kept short-circuited when stored. Capacitors built into equipment which is not in use must similarly be short-circuited individually, otherwise hazard may exist when they are connected in series or if there is a circuit fault when in parallel.

It is recommended that all such capacitors should carry a label adjacent to their terminals, e.g.

> **WARNING**
> Keep short-circuited
> when not in use.

For the advice of the A.S.E. on electrical safety see *Education in Science*, 1979, 83, pp. 20–21.

Radioactivity

The use of radioactive materials in schools and educational establishments in England and Wales is governed by Administrative Memorandum 2/76. This Memorandum and its associated notes for guidance are essential reading for any teacher who wishes to undertake work with radioactive substances in a school, an establishment of further education or a college of education.

The provisions of Administrative Memorandum 2/76 replace those of the earlier Memorandum, 1/65. Teachers in Scotland are referred to S.E.D. Circulars, Nos. 689, 852 and 882.

In England and Wales, the approval of the Secretary of State is *not required* for work with the following, provided that certain conditions are fulfilled. These conditions, which are elaborated in the Memorandum, relate to the amounts of radioactive materials which may be stored, used or disposed of as waste.

1 The elements uranium, thorium, potassium and rubidium and those of their compounds which are available through the normal chemical suppliers.
2 Equipment containing radioactive sources with activities of the order of 3.7 kBq or less.
3 Luminous painted surfaces which have protective coverings and which comply with the relevant parts of the Radioactive Substances (Luminous Articles) Exemption Order 1962.

The approval of the Secretary of State is required for all other work with radioactive materials. There are two categories of approval, A and B, the latter relating to potentially less hazardous work. Advice on Category B work is given in the *Notes for the guidance of schools, establishments of further education and colleges of education on the use of radioactive substances and equipment producing X-rays*, H.M.S.O., 1976. Teachers with approval for work in category A are referred to the *Code of Practice for the protection of persons exposed to ionizing radiations in research and teaching*. Each of the two principal categories, A and B, for which approval is required, is divided into three sub-categories. Within each of these categories and sub-categories certain types of open and/or closed sources are permitted. Full details are given in the Memorandum, which also specifies the qualifications required by teachers who wish to work with radioactive materials, other than those for which approval is not required.

Teachers will wish to note the following points from the Memorandum.

1 Where classes include pupils below the age of sixteen, the use of ionizing radiations requiring the approval of the Secretary of State must consist of demonstration only.
2 Pupils below the age of sixteen must not be allowed in laboratories where older pupils are conducting experiments with ionizing radiations except when specifically approved closed sources with an activity of less than 370 kBq are being used.
3 Particular provisions are made for student teachers on teaching practice. The sources to be used must be closed sources relevant to work in category B3, unless the student teacher is qualified for work with ionizing radiations in another category. The Memorandum states the kinds and levels of qualification required for work in each category. In addition, the consent of the head of the establishment in which the teaching practice is undertaken must be obtained before the student teacher begins work with ionizing radiations in that establishment. A member of the science staff of a school must be present when a student teacher is using radioactive materials and all such materials brought by a student teacher to the school or college must be returned by him/her to the training establishment.

The following guidelines are suggested for working with materials of low activity in a school laboratory:

1 The normal laboratory rules (no eating, smoking etc.) must be rigorously followed.
2 A laboratory coat or other suitable protective clothing should

always be worn. If possible, it should be kept for work with radioactive material but in any case must be monitored at the end of each working session. It should be kept in the laboratory.

3 Hands must be scrupulously washed and monitored after each practical class. Disposable towels should be used.

4 The radioactive sources must not be allowed to come into contact with the skin.

5 Mouth operations (pipetting, licking labels etc.) are forbidden.

6 Protective gloves (disposable polythene are convenient) should be worn.

7 If possible, a working area should be set aside for exclusive use with radioactive sources. The most practical procedure is often to confine such work to a series of large plastic trays lined with paper towels.

8 Glassware for use with radioactive sources should be kept solely for such use and stored separately.

9 It is essential to check the quantity of radioactive materials, whether these are stored or being disposed of, at the end of a practical class.

10 It is advisable to label bottles etc. containing radioactive material with an appropriate warning notice. The recognized symbol for radiation is a black trefoil on a yellow background. Rolls of adhesive tape bearing this symbol and the legend 'radioactive' are readily purchased from the usual laboratory suppliers.

Teachers should also read the following publication of the National Radiological Protection Board:

T. G. Williams, *The Use of Plutonium-239 Sources in Schools and other educational establishments*, H.M.S.O., 1974.

Ultra-violet radiation

Ultra-violet radiation lies in the band of wavelength between 10 and 400 nm. The action of such radiation on the eye is acute, being absorbed by the outer layers, the cornea and conjunctiva. Conjunctivitis results four to eight days after the exposure and lasts for several days.

Ultra-violet lamps should always be properly shielded and eye protection worn if the source is exposed. No source should be viewed directly.

Note that an electric arc produces a large amount of ultra-violet light and is as dangerous as an open source. For a detailed review of the biological effects of ultra-violet radiation and of the maximum permissible exposures, see Hughes, D., *Hazards of Occupational Exposure to Ultra-violet Radiation*, University of Leeds, 1978.

Lasers

The name 'laser' is derived from the term Light Amplification by Stimulated Emission of Radiation. Lasers are being used to an increasing extent in rapidly widening fields of application.

The very short concentrated pulse of light can cause very severe eye damage, e.g. irradiation of the cornea first kills the outer surface epithelial cells, which slough off after a few hours giving rise to an excruciatingly painful eye condition. When a light pulse from a laser system enters the lens of the eye, it is concentrated on the retina where tissue may be destroyed to give a permanent blind spot.

Animal experiments show that retinal damage begins at about 10^{-2} joule cm^{-2} *received on the retina*. The focusing of parallel light by the eye lens can result in the intensity of the light incident on the retina being 10^6 times greater than that received on the pupil. Thus, unless other special factors are operating, the maximum laser energy density at the pupil of the eye should not exceed 10^{-9} joule cm^{-2} ($\equiv$ 10 μJ m^{-2}), (including a safety factor of 10).

Remember:

1 Any light reflecting surface will reflect laser pulses.
2 Work with lasers should be carried out in brightly lit rooms to avoid enlarging the pupils of the eyes.
3 Warning notices should be posted where lasers are being used.
4 Personnel in the area should stand behind the laser and at right angles to the proposed path of the beam before firing.
5 The danger area should be 'fenced off' and a warning notice set up.
6 All workers *regularly* associated with laser systems are recommended to have a periodic ophthalmological examination.
7 The laser source should be rigidly fixed so that the direction of the beam cannot be inadvertently altered.

The use of lasers in schools in England and Wales is governed by Administrative Memorandum 7/70, *The Use of Lasers in Schools*, and in Scotland by Circular 766, (1970), *Use of Lasers in Schools, Colleges of Education and Further Education Establishments*.

Photographic darkrooms

Since much of the work done in a photographic darkroom is conducted in complete or semi-darkness, design features are of particular importance. Cupboards should be fitted with sliding rather than swing doors and materials must not be stored on the floor. The floor must be made of non-slip material and be resistant to the chemicals used in photographic processing. Proper precautions must be taken in using these chemicals which can cause skin irritation and dermatitis and many of which are toxic. They must be kept away from the skin and polythene or rubber gloves are recommended. Tongs should be used to handle the photographic material being processed.

Good ventilation, not less than eight changes of air per hour, is essential in a darkroom. Note that some colour processing techniques require the use of a hooded fume extractor.

Where a large darkroom is to be used simultaneously by more than one worker, broad white lines should be painted on the walls at eye level to provide a guide to change of direction.

Darkrooms are normally fitted with a conventional white light to allow the room to be cleaned. This should be operated via a key switch to prevent accidental illumination of the darkroom. Safety lights should be operated by pull-switches conveniently placed in relation to the working area.

Noise

Noise is a much underestimated hazard. It is well known that sudden and loud sounds can cause damage to hearing but it is not generally appreciated that continuous and prolonged exposure to quite low noise levels may produce a similar effect. Because of the gradual and insidious effect of low noise levels, impairment of hearing may be unrecognized for many years.

The effect of noise on hearing depends upon the frequency band in which the sound is being transmitted. However, chronic exposure to sound intensity 85–90 dB above the threshold of hearing on the dBA scale may have an adverse effect on hearing. Hence, everything should be done to reduce the level of noise in science laboratories and classrooms, consistent with safety. For example, roaring bunsen flames should be moderated and excessively noisy fume cupboard motors should receive attention. Attention is drawn to the *Code of practice for reducing the exposure of employed persons to noise*, issued by the Department of Employment and the advice given in *Noise and the Worker*, published on behalf of the Health and Safety Executive.

3 Biological hazards

Work in the biological sciences raises a number of unique safety issues in addition to those associated with the use of chemical materials or electrical apparatus. These include the handling and disposal of micro-organisms, the problems of maintaining and utilizing living material, the organization of field work and the personal nature of some biological knowledge which can cause distress in individual children.

Microbiological hazards

Work with micro-organisms now forms an integral part of many school science curricula. An increasing number and variety of bacteria are being produced during school bacteriological studies. An American survey in 1964–5 on the causal factors of accidental infection in micro-biological laboratories showed that 80% of infections were caused by unsafe acts that occurred without realization or recognition, resulting in the release of undetected amounts of micro-organisms into the environment.

The principal hazards when working with micro-organisms are as follows.

1 Micro-organisms which enter the body may multiply rapidly and to such an extent that the normal defence mechanisms against secondary infection become inadequate.

2 The metabolism of micro-organisms may produce toxins, some of which are highly dangerous.

3 Some micro-organisms, notably bacteria, are capable of rapid mutation to generate species which may be highly pathogenic. Thus *Staphylococcus aureus* has been shown to mutate to drug-resistant pathogenic varieties and *Serratia marcescens* readily produces strains which are resistant to antibiotics and which are associated with serious illness.

4 Individuals vary widely in their susceptibility to infection so that a

particular micro-organism may pose a significant hazard to one person in a class but not to the remainder.

5 The susceptibility of an individual to infection by a particular species will vary from time to time and will be lower immediately after illness or treatment with some drugs.

6 Some micro-organisms stimulate an allergic reaction which may be manifest by a variety of unpleasant symptoms.

7 Cultures of non-pathogenic organisms may become contaminated with other species. The fungus *Aspergillus* is a common source of such contamination and a species such as *Aspergillus flavus* is dangerously pathogenic.

It follows, therefore, that ALL CULTURES MUST BE TREATED AS POTENTIALLY HAZARDOUS.

The following bacteria and fungi are among those used in schools and present a minimum degree of risk if the proper procedure is followed.

Bacteria	Fungi
Acetobacter aceti	*Agaricus bisporus*
Bacillus subtilis	*Aspergillus nidulans*
Chromobacterium lividum	*Aspergillus niger*
Erwinia carotovora	*Botrytis cinerea*
Escherichia coli	*Chaetomium globosum*
Micrococcus luteus	*Coprinus lagopus*
Pseudomonas fluorescens	*Fusarium solani*
Rhizobium leguminosarum	*Mucor hiemalis*
Spirillum serpens	*Mucor mucedo*
Staphylococcus albus	*Penicillium chrysogenum*
Staphylococcus epidermidis	*Penicillium notatum*
Streptomyces griseus	*Phycomyces blakesleanus*
Vibrio natriegens	*Phytophthora infestans*
	Pythium debaryanum
	Rhizopus sexualis
	Rhizopus stolonifer
	Saccharomyces cerevisiae
	Saccharomyces ellipsoides
	Saprolegnia litoralis
	Schizosaccharomyces pombe
	Sordaria Fimicola

Where cultures of specific micro-organisms are required they must be obtained only from recognized suppliers. The following micro-organisms should *not* be used in courses taught to pupils below the age of 16 years.

Chromobacterium violaceum	*Pseudomonas tabacci*
Clostridium perfringens	*Serratia marcescens*
Pseudomonas aeruginosa	*Staphylococcus aureus*
Pseudomonas solanacearum	*Xanthomonas phaseoli*

Note also the recommendation of the D.E.S. that 'anaerobic culture is best avoided in elementary courses' because of the danger of isolating anaerobic pathogens. For further advice on micro-organisms suitable for use in school science teaching, see D.E.S., *The use of micro-organisms in schools*, Education Pamphlet No. 61, 1977; Holt, G., 'Practical tips for the safe handling of micro-organisms in schools', *School Science Review*, 1974, **56**, 195, pp. 248–252 and Fry, P., *Micro-organisms*, Schools Council Educational Use of Living Organisms Project, 1977. For a list of highly dangerous pathogens which must not be used in schools, see D.E.S., Administrative Memorandum 6/76, *The Laboratory Use of Dangerous Pathogens*, (Welsh Office 4/76). Teachers in doubt about the hazards associated with a particular micro-organism should not undertake work with that species until advice has been obtained from the Microbiology in Schools Advisory Committee at the Polytechnic of Central London or from the Secretary of the Dangerous Pathogens Advisory Group (Alexander Fleming House, London SE1 6JE). For a list of sources of local advice, see *J.Biol. Ed.*, 1979, **13**, 2, pp. 156–158.

Correct technique is of paramount important when working with micro-organisms. All 'hand-to-mouth' operations should be prohibited, including the moistening of labels with the tongue and the use of mouth-operated pipettes. All exposed cuts should be protected with sterile, waterproof dressings. Benches should be swabbed with industrial methylated spirit before and after practical work. Wherever possible, a transfer chamber should be used to reduce the risk of contaminating both a culture and the laboratory. Note that aerosols, perhaps the commonest means of contamination, may be formed by the spluttering of an inoculating loop during flame-sterilization. This may be avoided by dipping the loop into 70% ethanol and draining it against the side of the container before inserting into the flame.

After inoculation, all plates must be sealed with tape and clearly labelled to indicate the date and nature of the inoculum. Cultures in

Petri dishes should be incubated in an inverted position to prevent any condensation from collecting upon the micro-organisms. In disposing of such condensates by pouring into a suitable disinfectant, it is essential to avoid the formation of an aerosol. Wherever possible, cultures should be incubated at ambient temperature rather than at 37 °C which tends to encourage the selection of organisms adapted to man's body temperature.

All cultured colonies must be rendered harmless before they are inspected by a class of pupils. This may be done by means of a swab of cotton wool soaked in freshly prepared 40% aqueous methanal (formaldehyde) left in position overnight. The swab is removed and the culture resealed with tape before inspection by the class.

Where a colony of micro-organisms is to be subjected to microscopic examination, an aqueous suspension of the colony should be prepared by the teacher. This is then treated with one or two drops of 40% aqueous methanal to kill the micro-organisms before samples are transferred to a microscope slide by means of a teat-pipette. Pupils should not make wet-mount preparations of living organisms.

Care is needed in the selection of a suitable culture medium. The D.E.S. advises that blood agar should not be used in elementary courses and that McConkey's bile salt medium should be used only when the teacher is satisfied that pupils have 'adequate experience in microbial techniques'. For advice on these techniques and on the culture and maintenance of a wide variety of living organisms see Archenhold, W. F., Jenkins, E. W., and Wood-Robinson, C. *op. cit.*, especially Chapters 8 and 9.

Unwanted cultures should be destroyed by autoclaving or rigorous chemical sterilization. Material for incineration should be placed in labelled plastic bags and burnt as soon as possible. Plastic Petri dishes are not designed for re-use and, after sterilization, must be discarded. Glassware should be autoclaved after immersion in a freshly prepared solution of sodium oxochlorate(I) (sodium hypochlorite). If autoclaving of contaminated glassware is not possible, at least 24 hours should be allowed for effective chemical sterilization. A 1% aqueous solution of sodium oxochlorate(I) may also be used to treat cultures spilled on the bench or elsewhere. Disposable gloves should be worn during this cleaning operation and contaminated clothing and equipment must be disinfected before being sent for laundering or washing.

A laboratory coat or some other suitable form of protective clothing is particularly important in microbiological work and such clothing should be left in the laboratory at the end of the class. Personal belongings must be kept off working surfaces and, as always, the rule prohibiting eating, drinking or smoking in a laboratory be observed strictly. Although it is sometimes convenient to store stock cultures at about 4 °C in a refrigerator, microbiological materials must not be placed in a refrigerator which is used for storing food.* Where stock cultures are maintained, a sub-culture must be plated out and examined for signs of contamination before the rest of the stock is used for further experiments. If there are signs of mixed growth in the sub-culture, the stock should be sterilized, discarded and replaced by fresh material.

After practical classes, hands must be washed thoroughly with an appropriate antiseptic and dried using individual paper towels rather than roller or other communal towels.

It should be noted that some practical microbiology texts intended or recommended for use in schools leave much to be desired from a safety point of view. For a review and recommendations, see Wyatt, H. V., Wright K. A., 'How Safe are Microbiology Texts?', *J. Biol. Ed.*, 1974, **8**, 4, pp. 216–218.

School laboratory animals

Over one hundred diseases of animals are known to be transmissible to man so that the maintenance of living animals in a school laboratory poses a health hazard as well as considerable organizational problems such as cleaning and feeding during the school holidays.

Animals must be kept in hygienic cages or aquaria which are of the correct design and size. School stocks of animals must be obtained from a reliable source. A list of reliable breeders of animals suitable for keeping in a school, together with information leaflets on animal care, may be obtained from the Universities' Federation for Animal Welfare (230 High Street, Potters Bar, Hertfordshire).

Although the importance of zoonoses must not be overemphasized in the school situation, it is important to remember that animals are liable to infections which could be passed on to pupils by bites, scratches, ectoparasites or inhalation of contaminated aerosols, dust or droplets.

The most common diseases which can be contracted are probably Salmonellosis (*Salmonella typhi-murium* and *S. enteriditis*), Staphylococcal infections and ringworm (*Trichophyton* sp.). Wild animals, dead or alive, should not be used for school work since they may well harbour zoonoses. This is especially true of rats, which may harbour, for example, ratbite fever (*Spirillum* sp.), Weil's disease (*Leptospira* sp.) and *Salmonella* spp., of rodents in general and of pigeons and hedgehogs.

* See also regrigerator fires (p. 52).

Abattoir material also needs to be used with care because of the possibility of infection with *Salmonella*. Such infection is also associated with tortoises, most reptiles and especially terrapins.

Budgerigars, pigeons, doves, parrots, and all species of native wild bird are susceptible to ornithosis (psittacosis), a disease which is transmissible to, and often fatal to man. On no account should monkeys or other imported wild mammals be kept in schools. As far as possible, animals should be removed from laboratories in which any microbiological work is to be carried out.

Advice on handling and maintaining living material in schools will be found in the following publications:

D.E.S., *Keeping Animals in Schools: a handbook for teachers*, H.M.S.O.

Schools Council, *Educational Use of Living Organisms Project:*
Animal Accommodation for Schools
Small Mammals
Organisms for Genetics
Micro-organisms
Plants

The Educational Use of Living Organisms: a source book, E.U.P., 1975

Schools Council, *Recommended practice for schools relating to the use of living organisms and material of living origin*, E.U.P., 1974

A.S.E., *Biology Teaching in Schools involving Experiment or Demonstration with Animals or Pupils*, 1972

For a detailed list of zoonoses, see: *Precautions against biological hazards*, Imperial College of Science and Technology, 1974, Appendix 2.

On no account should animals kept as pets be used for dissection nor should animals bred for dissection in a school be allowed to become pets. All animals, or parts of animals, used for dissection must be free from disease and the number dissected should be the minimum consistent with the achievement of the educational aims. Wherever possible and appropriate, prepared specimens, models and other aids should be used to supplement or partially substitute for, dissection. Pupils must be taught proper techniques for using dissecting instruments and be made fully aware of the hazards they present. All such instruments must be cleaned thoroughly and sterilized immediately after completion of the dissection exercise. For recommendations on the conduct of dissection in schools, see the report on the *Dissection of Animals in Schools*, prepared by the joint Biological Education Committee of the Royal Society and Institute of Biology (1976).

**Field work and
educational visits**

The organization of field work poses a number of problems for the teacher. Clearly different problems arise if the work is to be conducted at a centre some distance from the school and over a period of several days. But, whatever the nature and duration of the work, it is ESSENTIAL to know the individual capabilities of the pupils involved and to be fully aware of all the hazards that the field environment, in the broadest sense of the term, presents. Wherever possible, a teacher should make a preliminary visit to the site of any field work, note any natural or other hazards and if appropriate estimate the significance of any likely changes in the weather.

Any field trip or visit should be recognized as an official school function and the teacher must be familiar with any regulations drawn up by the L.E.A. (or other employing body) about the size and insurance of school parties.

For most outdoor activities, a 'recall procedure' is essential and the recall signal must be fully understood and obeyed promptly by all members of a group. Precise and unambiguous instructions for a rendezvous are also necessary and each member of a group must be told, in advance, what to do if he or she becomes separated from the main party and 'lost'. Adequate first-aid equipment is essential. However, note that a trivial accident on a lonely moorland or mountain site causes much greater disruption than a similar incident in the classroom or laboratory; and, in these circumstances, a teacher is unlikely to have access to expert, medical help should this be required. Some Local Authorities require teachers in charge of out-of-school visits to hold a recognized first-aid qualification but every teacher in charge of a group of pupils must possess basic first-aid skills. These include the care of wounds and the control of bleeding, a technique for artificial respiration, the treatment of shock and the transport of an injured or sick person to a place where professional medical help is available. For advice on first aid, see Chapter 5.

Teachers contemplating school outings are strongly urged to consult the following publication:

Schools Council, *Out and About: A teacher's guide to safety on educational visits*. Evans/Methuen Educational 1972.

Attention is drawn below to some common situations in which personal injury may be sustained if proper precautions are not taken.

The exploration of rough country and steep slopes

Upland and mountain terrain should be treated with respect. What appears an innocuous slope in warm sunshine can, within an hour, be converted by a sudden weather change into a death trap for the unprepared.

Before setting out, ensure that **everyone** is fit enough to undertake the exercise, is properly equipped, has a reserve of warm clothing and some emergency rations and that someone in the party has a map, compass and first-aid kit.

Do not risk being benighted on a mountain, and have a whistle or an electric torch (with fresh batteries) to signal with in case you miscalculate distances or time.

In general young persons are physiologically *and* psychologically less resilient than healthy adults and a suitable safety margin must be allowed. A particular pitfall to avoid is the confusion of muscular development with physical fitness for a particular exercise. Suitable preparation might include simulation or practice exercises.

People living in lowland or urban conditions must be taught that torrent-tracked streams can rise very rapidly in level, bringing down rock as a result of heavy rain in the upper catchment areas. Camping sites should take account of this fact.

Beware of falling rocks and try to avoid dislodging stones: there may be someone below you. A small stone has a lethal momentum after it has fallen a few hundred feet.

Glaciers, rock faces, mines, caves, open water etc. should be attempted ONLY under an experienced leader and after suitable training exercises.

For detailed advice on the preparation for, and conduct of, such activities, see D.E.S., *Safety in Outdoor Pursuits*, H.M.S.O., 1977.

Seaside locations

Marshland and tidal saltings should be traversed only after taking local advice. The tide comes in over many salt marshes almost as fast as a man can run.

Living in tents and caravans

Ensure that fire buckets are filled and placed at strategic points and that sanitary arrangements conform to the highest possible standards of hygiene. In particular, attention must be given to the siting of latrines and the disposal of waste and rubbish.

Forest and heath areas

In forest and heath areas and where agricultural crops are ripening, take particular care to avoid starting fires, e.g. by carelessly discarded cigarette ends, inefficiently extinguished camp fires, etc.

Walking in narrow lanes

In narrow country lanes, do not straggle in the roadway: the motorist is not expecting you or your pupils near the crown of the road. If walking on the roads at night or at dusk cannot be avoided, the leader and rearguard of the party should wear distinctive clothing and carry appropriate lights.

Industrial visits

Many schools now arrange for their pupils industrial visits of a day or half-day's duration. In addition, it is increasingly common to find pupils, individually, or in small groups, spending much longer periods of time in industry as part of a programme of 'work experience' or a schools industry link scheme. In all these situations, it is essential to determine and agree, in advance, the allocation of responsibility for the supervision of pupils at all times and to ensure that everyone involved is fully aware of the hazards presented by the industrial environment and of the safety rules devised to contain them. Note that there are legal restrictions on the employment in industry of pupils below the statutory school-leaving age and that it may be necessary to arrange special insurance cover to protect such pupils participating in work experience schemes. For further advice, see Schools Council, *op. cit.*, 1972, Chapter 5.

The personal nature of biological knowledge

In the biological sciences, some teaching situations can cause emotional distress to individual pupils. It is the teacher's responsibility to prevent such situations from arising. Stressful incidents include distress (even fainting) at the dissection of a freshly killed animal and the individual upset of a child discovering that he or she is adopted or illegitimate as a result of class studies of inheritance of eye colour.

Many physiological experiments will actually involve the pupils themselves and great discretion is needed in publicly discussing individual variations within a class.

The use of pupils as the subjects of experiments raises complex legal, as well as moral and educational issues. Where such experiments involve procedures beyond the normal everyday experience of pupils, teachers must explain fully the precautions to be taken and must ensure pupils understand the reasons for them. The following guidelines should be observed.

1 No pressure must be brought to bear upon a pupil to urge him/her to become the subject of an experiment.
2 No chemical should be swallowed.
3 The advice of a School Medical Officer should be sought before conducting any experiment which involves the tasting of any substance other than conventional foodstuffs or a common substance, e.g. sodium chloride, known to be safe in the quantities to be used. Note that the tasting of phenylthiourea (phenylthiocarbamide) or PTC involves a number of hazards. Paper strips, containing no more than 0.1 mg of PTC, should be used and no pupil should be allowed to taste more than two strips. The strips must not be taken out of the laboratory and pupils must not have access to the solid or a stock solution which should be kept in a locked poisons cupboard.
4 Medical advice should also be sought before undertaking any experiment involving an unusual degree of physical or physiological stress. Particular attention should be given to the needs of epileptic or asthmatic pupils.
5 Procedures such as blood sampling should be carried out only under sterile conditions and only with the approval of a medical officer; such sampling carries the risk of transmitting infective hepatitis unless sterile procedures are guaranteed. The procedures recommended by the A.S.E. are reproduced as Appendix A.
6 Prior parental consent is generally advisable for all experiments involving pupils as the subjects of experiment. However, it should be recognized that a pupil is unlikely to become involved in such an experiment with a full knowledge of the possible hazards and the D.E.S. comments that 'teachers may consider it advisable to avoid all such experiments with pupils below the age of 16 years'.
7 On no account should an experiment be performed which involves the deliberate contamination of a pupil with micro-organisms.
8 On no account should any experiments be conducted or demonstrated in which drugs or other means are used to influence the mental state of a pupil or teacher and teachers are strongly advised not to perform experiments involving the use of an electroencephalograph to study 'biological feedback'.

Abnormal susceptibilities of individuals

Haemophilia

Teachers must be informed, at the earliest opportunity, of any pupil who suffers from haemophilia.

Colour blindness

All persons working in a school should ensure that they are aware of any abnormality in their colour vision. If any abnormality exists, it should be reported to the teacher who may need to take steps to overcome resulting difficulties.

Epilepsy

Teachers or pupils in their charge who suffer from epilepsy are not barred from working in laboratories. It is, however, ESSENTIAL that the teacher be aware of any such disabilities and knows how to deal with an attack suffered by one of his pupils.

Note that an epileptic attack can be induced by the use of stroboscopic lighting of a critical frequency. The phenomenon is imperfectly understood but teachers must be aware of this hazard and take appropriate precautions where necessary.

A major fit can be frightening in appearance, especially to anyone seeing an attack of epilepsy for the first time. Keep calm and remember that the first requirement is to prevent the victim from hurting himself. Do not restrain convulsive movements but gently guide the victim away from hard objects on which he could suffer injury. Loosen the tie, collar or other tight clothing and cradle the patient's head in the arms. If an opportunity arises, gently insert the corner of a clean, folded handkerchief between the victim's teeth so as to prevent the tongue and lips from being bitten.

There are approximately 100 000 children in Britain who have epileptic disorders. Of these, some 60 000 attend ordinary schools and are more likely to suffer minor rather than major attacks of epilepsy. These minor attacks are of three types, although a child can have more than one type of epilepsy.

Minor motor seizures are characterized by involuntary movements of any part of the body, e.g. an arm, finger or an entire side. These seizures may last for a few seconds only but may also develop into a major epileptic fit ('grand mal').

Petit mal attacks are often very difficult to detect in the classroom or laboratory situation. A pupil may have a vacant or blank stare, may stumble, have a brief 'black-out' lasting for a second or so or simply be unable to hear what is being said to him. Petit mal attacks may occur many times during the course of a school day.

Psychomotor attacks are manifest by behaviour which is suddenly irrational or inappropriate to the circumstances in which the person finds himself, e.g. a pupil may smack his lips repeatedly or get up and run around the laboratory. When the attack has passed, the individual will not know what has happened during the seizure.

Further information and advice is obtainable from the British Epilepsy Association (3–6 Alfred Place, London WC1E 7ED), which publishes a helpful leaflet entitled *A Teacher's Guide to Epilepsy*.

Allergy and hypersensitivity

The skin may be adversely affected by contact with chemical reagents which cause an allergic reaction. Although only a small proportion of the school population will be susceptible to any particular allergen, individual instances are none the less distressing. Allergic reactions are often associated with biological materials. The coats of laboratory animals, *Primula* and *Pelargonium* spp., grasses and some fungi have all been cited as sources of allergens. The giant hogweed, *Heracleum mantegazzianum*, has sap containing a substance which in contact with the skin and in sunlight causes exaggerated sunburn reaction.

The stem, leaves, flower heads and sap of daffodils, hyacinths, jonquils, narcissi and tulips may act as irritants causing painful lesions on the fingers. The cowslip, *Primula veris*, has been known to cause dermatitis and the common houseplant *Primula obconica* has pollen and glandular hairs which contain an irritant poison. Many members of the ivy family, especially the poison ivy, *Rhus toxicodendron*, are known to contain an irritant sap.

A note on allergy to locusts is available from the Anti-Locust Research Centre, College House, Wright's Lane, London W.8.

An individual may be hypersensitive to substances in the vapour, liquid or solid state and a number of compounds can cause dermatitis if brought into contact with some skins. The compounds which are most frequently responsible for dermatitis belong to the following groups: hydrocarbons, chlorinated hydrocarbons, nitro-chlorohydrocarbons and phenols.

Such individuals must take special precautions, e.g. wear protective gloves or use suitable barrier creams.

Note that exposure to a substance of biological or chemical origin, even in a dose as low as 10^{-9}g, may cause serious damage to body proteins. Such a small, initial 'sensitizing' dose may produce no observable effects but subsequent exposure to an even smaller 'challenging' dose can cause a virulent reaction and severe tissue damage. 'Cross-sensitization' of the skin is also possible, i.e. exposure to one substance may render the skin susceptible to challenging doses of a larger number of chemically-related materials.

1-bromo-2, 4-dinitrobenzene is a powerful contact sensitizer sometimes used in school science teaching and, as with the corresponding chloro- and fluoro- derivatives, precautions against skin contact, inhalation and ingestion are essential. Attention is drawn to the recommendation of the D.E.S. that 'teachers should not use chemicals with which they are unfamiliar, especially biochemicals, unless they have been given authoritative advice about them. Such advice can be obtained from the Regional Medical Services Adviser of the Department of Employment'.

Insecticides and pesticides

Insecticides, fungicides and weedkillers are three classes of substance likely to be found in school biology laboratories or greenhouses. These substances are often very toxic in higher than the recommended concentrations and for some, e.g. paraquat, there is no known antidote. Such material must therefore be securely stored, adequately labelled and properly used.

At least twenty deaths in Britain in the past fifteen years are known to have been caused by paraquat. In almost all the cases, death followed the decanting of paraquat solutions into soft drink bottles.

As a result, the sale of paraquat in the United Kingdom is now subject to strict controls. The substance is included in Part 2 of the Poisons list and may be sold only by authorized persons who will require the purchaser to countersign an entry in a Poisons Book. However, these controls do not apply to preparations containing less than 5% of paraquat.

Almost all the pesticides supplied for sale within the United Kingdom are now 'approved' under the Pesticides Safety Precautions Scheme, a voluntary agreement between the agrochemical industry and the government. However, many chemicals 'cleared' under this scheme are intended for professional use in agriculture, forestry and horticulture and, as such, these substances should not be used on an 'amateur' basis in school science teaching.

The use of the letter 'A' as displayed on small containers of garden pesticides indicates that the Ministry of Agriculture has been satisfied that the substance concerned fulfils its stated function and is *safe when used as directed*. As with all pesticides and insecticides, the detailed instructions supplied with the product must be observed scrupulously.

Seeds supplied to schools are occasionally dressed with a protective coating of fungicide/insecticide. Such seeds should not be handled unnecessarily by pupils or teachers and, wherever possible, untreated seed should be used. If it is essential to work with treated seed, the hands should be washed immediately after use. Note that plant or other material collected 'in the field' may contain or be coated with toxic pesticide or other material.

For advice on the storage, use and disposal of pesticides, together with lists of pesticides scheduled as poisons or recommended to be so, see *Education in Science*, 1979, 85, pp. 26–28.

Poisonous plants

Poisoning by plant material is usually associated with younger pupils, although cases of older children being poisoned in this way have been reported.

The range of toxic plant material is much greater than is commonly realized although, in some cases, only part of a plant may be dangerous, and the hazards associated with some garden plants are not as widely recognized as they should be. The following Table lists some of the more common toxic species of plant material.

Common name	Botanical name	Poisonous parts
GARDEN FLOWERS		
Aconite (winter)	*Eranthis hyemalis*	All
Christmas Rose	*Helleborus niger*	All
Foxglove	*Digitalis purpurea*	All
Iris (Blue Flag)	*Iris versicolor*	All
Larkspur	*Delphinium ajacis*	Foliage and seeds
Lily of the Valley	*Convallaria majalis*	All
Lupin	*Lupinus* sp.	All
Monkshood	*Aconitum anglicum*	All
Narcissus (Daffodil, Jonquil)	*Narcissus* sp.	Bulbs
GARDEN VEGETABLES		
Potato	*Solanum tuberosum*	Green sprouting tubers and leaves
Rhubarb	*Rheum rhaponticum*	Leaves
SHRUBS AND TREES		
Broom	*Cytisus (Sarothamnus) scoparius*	Seeds
Cherry laurel	*Prunus laurocerasus*	All
Laburnum (Golden Rain)	*Laburnum anagyroides*	All
Rhododendron	Species: *Azalea* American laurel Mountain laurel	Leaves and flowers
Yew	*Taxus baccata*	All; seeds lethal
Snowberry	*Symphoricarpus albus*	Fruits

Common name	Botanical name	Poisonous parts
HEDGEROW PLANTS		
Black Nightshade	*Solanum nigrum*	All
Buttercups	*Ranunculus* sp.	Sap
Deadly Nightshade	*Atropa belladonna*	All
Privet	*Ligustrum vulgaris*	Berries
Thorn Apple	*Datura stramonium*	All
MARSHLAND PLANTS		
Hemlock	*Conium maculatum*	All
Hemlock, Water Dropwort	*Oenanthe crocata*	All
Kingcup, Marsh Marigold	*Caltha palustris*	Sap
HOUSE PLANTS		
Castor Oil Plant	*Ricinus communis*	Seeds
Dumb Cane	*Diffenbachia* sp.	All
Hyacinth	*Hyacinthus* sp.	Bulbs
Poinsettia	*Euphorbia pulcherrima*	Leaves and flowers
WOODLAND PLANTS		
Cuckoo Pint (Wild Arum)	*Arum maculatum*	All
Mistletoe	*Viscum album*	Fruits
Oak	*Quercus* sp.	Fruits and leaves
Poison ivy	*Rhus toxicodendron*	All
Toadstools	*Amanita muscaria* *A. pantherina* *A. phalloides*	All

For fuller details, see:

Ministry of Agriculture, Fisheries and Food, *British Poisonous Plants*, 1968.

North, P., *Poisonous Plants and Fungi*, 1967.

Imperial College of Science and Technology, *Precautions against Biological Hazards*, 1974, pp. 103–104.

Symposium on Carcinogens of Plant Origin, *Cancer Research*, 11, **28**, 1968, p. 2233, *et seq.*

4 Fire

PRECAUTIONS AGAINST THE OUTBREAK OF FIRE

General

1 Control the potential fuel supply

This may be done by the selection for use of non-flammable materials, materials of low combustibility, fire-proofed materials etc. or by limiting the amount of flammable materials in any specific location which has not been designed and designated for their storage.

Attention is drawn to the D.E.S. Building Bulletin No. 7, *Fire and the Design of Schools*, H.M.S.O., 1975.

2 Limit the supply of oxygen (air)

Positive limitation of oxygen as a means of fire prevention is normally available only in industrial or laboratory situations. The exclusion of the oxygen support medium is, however, an important fire extinguishing method. KEEP FIRE STOP DOORS CLOSED. Do not leave them fixed open. Fire stop doors limit the flow of air to a fire.

3 Heat limitation

Care in preventing the overheating of combustible materials is a fundamental fire precaution. Any form of intense radiant heat whether direct or as a result of the focusing effect of an intermediate transparent object should be avoided. Overloading of electrical circuits leads to overheating and fire risk as does the careless use of smoking materials.

The nature of fire

There are three essential factors, sometimes called 'the fire triangle', which must be present before a fire can break out: remove one of these three factors and the fire will go out. The control of these three essentials is the basis of all fire prevention and control.

The three essential factors are:

1 A source of FUEL.
2 OXYGEN, usually from the air but also from certain chemicals, to act as a SUPPORT MEDIUM.
3 HEAT sufficient to bring the fuel to a temperature at which sustained combustion can be initiated (the ignition temperature).

The fire triangle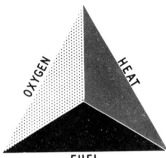

Fire is a self-sustaining combustion process which takes place in the vapour phase, producing heat and smoke or incandescence or all three. If the heat generated raises the temperature sufficiently, non-flammable materials may decompose and in doing so produce noxious or toxic decomposition products and perhaps lead to structural collapse. Solids usually need to be heated to a point at which they give off flammable vapour before they will ignite but many organic solvents are sufficiently volatile to give off flammable vapours and be a fire hazard well below normal air temperatures (see note on refrigerator fires, p. 52 and p. 62).

Below the self-ignition temperature of a combustible mixture a source of ignition is normally necessary to initiate combustion. The nature of the chemical processes involved is such that ignition may result from an extremely short burst of energy, e.g. an electric spark.

Laboratory fire risk reduction

Solvent supplies in laboratories should be kept to a minimum, preferably not more than will be needed during the current working day. Not more than 500 cm³ of any one volatile, flammable liquid should be kept in bottles on laboratory benches or shelves and all such bottles must be clearly labelled 'Highly Flammable'.

Solvents not required during the current working day should be kept in the departmental solvent store.

Solvents not in immediate use should be kept in a specially designed solvent storage cupboard.

Used solvents should be placed in the waste solvent container(s) for recovery or disposal. These solvents should be collected and put in a safe place daily. There are severe penalties for the contravention of the stringent requirements of the *Control of Pollution Act* (1974). For advice, see page 18.

Solvents MUST NOT BE PUT DOWN THE DRAIN. This practice is both a serious explosion hazard and a contravention of the Public Health Acts.

Refrigerator fires. Solvents MUST NOT be placed in refrigerators in open containers. Explosive concentrations of vapour/air mixtures can form from very small amounts of solvent, which may be ignited by sparks from micro switches and thermostats. New refrigerators for laboratory use should have all spark sources placed outside the cold chamber.

TYPES OF FIRE EXTINGUISHING EQUIPMENT

**Water
extinguishers**

This group extinguish by the cooling action of the water. **Hose reels** are normally connected to the mains supply, which is turned on as the hose reel is unwound.

In an automatic hose reel there are three water control valves:

  (i) a main stop-cock which is normally locked in the open position by means of a leather strap;
 (ii) a main control valve, within the axle of the hose reel, which opens when the hose is unreeled, and
(iii) a manual control valve on the nozzle.

Important. After use, the hose should be rewound by turning the reel until the main valve is closed. This may leave some hose still unreeled. Wind this on by hand. DO NOT FORCE THE REEL or permanent damage to the expensive main control valve will result.

Soda acid extinguishers usually contain 2 gallons ($\cong$ 9 l) of a solution of sodium bicarbonate (hydrogencarbonate) in water. When

**Soda acid
extinguisher**

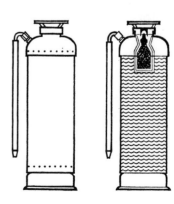

actuated, sulphuric acid from a built-in container reacts with the solution, carbon dioxide is released and forces a jet of solution through the nozzle. (Cannot be turned off.)

Carbon-dioxide expelled water extinguishers usually contain 2 gallons of water expelled in a jet when a built-in cylinder of carbon dioxide is punctured. (This jet cannot be turned off.)

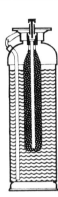

CO_2 expelled water extinguisher

Foam extinguishers

Foam extinguishers contain aqueous solutions of foaming agents which mix and react to produce large amounts of stable foam. (They cannot be turned off.)

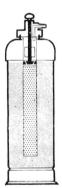

Foam extinguisher

This group acts mainly by excluding air from the fuel. There is some slight cooling effect also.

Carbon dioxide extinguishers

This type acts by excluding oxygen. Being denser than air a blanket of CO_2 gas forms over the fuel. There is no cooling effect.

Carbon dioxide extinguishers consist of a cylinder containing carbon dioxide at high pressure. The cylinder is fitted with a plastic horn to direct the jet of gas. N.B. The hand MUST NOT be in contact with the horn when in use.

The jet of gas is extremely cold and when emitted freezes water vapour in the air causing ice to form on the horn. (The white cloud formed consists of ice crystals and solid carbon dioxide.)

This type has a very short duration of action and is trigger operated.

CO_2 extinguisher

Vaporizing liquid extinguishers

These act in a similar manner to the CO_2 extinguishers but are more effective due to the higher vapour density.

Carbon tetrachloride (CTC) extinguishers are now obsolete. This type of extinguisher should be withdrawn from use, even on motor vehicles where they will only be used in the open air. Carbon tetrachloride and its decomposition products are highly toxic. These extinguishers operate by a pump action.

BCF type extinguishers are usually supplied in pressurized containers, the liquid in the container vaporizing on release of the pressure. The vapour is much denser than air and blankets the fire. BCF (bromochlorodifluoromethane) vapour is inert and of high density; it can however decompose on heating to give highly irritant, corrosive fumes.

Powder extinguishers

These extinguishers blanket the fire in an inert powder, i.e. exclude oxygen.

Dry sand is applied by shovel from a sand bucket.

Dry chemical. The powder is usually sodium bicarbonate (hydrogencarbonate) with additives to prevent caking. The powder is expelled under pressure by carbon dioxide. (They cannot be turned off.)

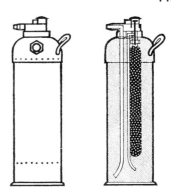

Powder extinguisher

Blankets

Extinguishing is by the mechanical smothering action of a non-combustible blanket.

Woven fibre-glass blankets are light in weight, flexible and can be re-used after cleaning.

Asbestos blankets are rather heavy and cumbersome. They may spread the fire if used on unstable containers of solvent, due to their lack of flexibility. They should no longer be used in schools.

N.B. A damp heavy woollen blanket can be used in some circumstances if it is remembered that on drying out the wool can ignite and smoulder.

Blankets are best used on small fires and in combination with an extinguisher.

Flammable liquid fires

The area of burning flammable liquid which different types of appliances will extinguish (when used by trained operators) is shown below.* Untrained operators may only be able to extinguish fires of approximately *half* the areas quoted. The areas quoted relate to contained fires.

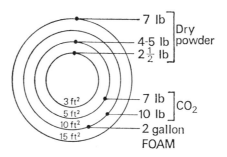

* At the time of writing, fire extinguishers are still calibrated in lb. 1 lb $\cong$ 0.45 kg and 1 ft $\cong$ 0.304 m.

CLASSIFICATION OF FIRES

The best method of fighting a fire depends upon the class to which the fire belongs: the wrong choice of extinguisher can intensify a fire or endanger the fire-fighter, e.g. by producing highly toxic fumes or causing the fire to flare up.

In the United Kingdom, fires in the past have been unofficially classified into four types A, B, C and D denoting respectively carbonaceous fires, flammable liquid fires, electrical fires and metal fires. Agreement has now been reached between European nations on a new classification which forms the subject of British Standard BS-EN 2: 1972 (formerly BS 4547: 1970) entitled *Classification of Fires*.

Class A Fires involving solid materials, normally of an organic nature, in which combustion generally occurs with the formation of glowing embers.

Class B Fires involving liquids or liquefiable solids.

Class C Fires involving gases or liquefied gases in the form of a liquid spillage, or a liquid or gas leak.

Class D Fires involving metals.

Note that electrical fires do not now constitute a class since any fire involving, or started by, electrical equipment must be a fire of Class A, B or D. For advice on dealing with electrical fires, see page 59.

CHOICE OF EXTINGUISHER

Class A fires
(paper, wood etc.)

Water is the best extinguishing agent, from either a hose-reel or a carbon-dioxide expelled water extinguisher. The hose-reel is to be preferred as the supply can be controlled.

Soda-acid extinguishers are an effective alternative but can do damage to property by staining and corrosion due to the effect of the acidic residue. However, any of the other types of extinguisher may be used if a water extinguisher is not available.

Class B fires
(fats, oils, solvents etc.)

Depending on the size and location of the fire the following extinguishers may be used:

(a) a fire blanket;

(b) a carbon dioxide extinguisher or, if appropriate, a vaporizing liquid extinguisher (BCF);

(c) a combination of (a) and (b);

(d) a foam extinguisher, directing the jet to the back of the fire and working forward towards the operator;

(e) a powder extinguisher, working from the periphery to the centre of the fire.

WARNING. DO NOT USE ANY WATER EXTINGUISHER ON CLASS B FIRES.

If a water extinguisher is used the burning liquid will float on the water and spread out, thus intensifying the fire as a result of the increase in surface exposed to the air. Flash evaporation of the water may cause the fire to erupt violently.

Class C fires
(gases, liquefied gases)

A foam or dry chemical powder extinguisher can be used to control fires involving shallow liquid spills. If gas cylinders are at risk from the heat of a fire, they may be cooled by spraying with water. Rubber tubing to gas burners should be inspected each term for signs of deterioration and particular care must be taken to ensure that all connections are secure and leakproof.

Class D fires
(metal)

A metal fire is a strongly exothermic reaction, usually with oxygen, but also with any suitably reactive gas, in which the heat of reaction raises the temperature of the metal to incandescence. The more finely divided the metal, i.e. the greater the surface to mass ratio, or the more reactive the metal, the greater the fire risk. Many metals which are of commercial use in the massive state are a hazard when in the powdered or finely divided form. Also many metals at high temperatures can react, explosively sometimes, with halogenated hydrocarbons, nitrogen, carbon dioxide or steam, thus limiting severely the available means of combating metal fires.

There are two basic methods of dealing with a metal fire:

(i) treat the reacting metal as a heat sink and control the subsequent fires due to ignition of other flammable materials, allowing the metal reaction to go to completion;

(ii) block the chemical reaction at the metal surface by cutting off the supply of support reactant, e.g. oxygen, using a suitable powder extinguisher.

Conventional extinguishers should NOT be used against metal fires. An appropriate dry powder should be kept available with a suitable means of application. Powdered talc, soda ash, limestone and dry sand are normally suitable for Class D fires. Special fusing powders are available for fires involving some metals, especially those which are radioactive.

N.B. Some metals when burning emit very dazzling light and coloured goggles should be kept at hand. Others, notably cadmium and mercury, produce highly toxic vapours when heated.

Electrical fires

First of all switch off the power (the source of heat). Then, if necessary, use a carbon dioxide or vaporizing liquid extinguisher (BCF). DO NOT USE WATER OR FOAM because of their electrical conductivity. REMEMBER, even if electrical equipment, e.g. TV set, refrigerator motor, is switched off, an electrical condenser can still administer a dangerous shock.

Powder extinguishers should only be used as a last resort; it is almost impossible to remove the finest powder from complicated equipment, e.g. switches and relays, during salvage operations.

REMEMBER: Although the primary task is to extinguish the fire the planning of fire precautions should always take into account salvage of the damaged items. A residue free, non-corrosive extinguishing agent is always to be preferred, particularly where delicate apparatus or materials may be present.

ACTION ON DISCOVERING A FIRE

Circumstances must dictate whether attacking a fire with portable first-aid fire-fighting equipment should take priority over summoning the fire brigade, raising the alarm etc. Clearly it is undesirable to allow a small fire to obtain a hold through summoning outside help but on the other hand it is dangerous to delay calling for assistance in dealing with any outbreak which may not be quickly extinguished by immediate personal action. Any fire which threatens to block an exit from a laboratory is to be regarded as very serious.

A fire should be attacked as soon as possible, provided that there is no personal danger in doing so. If attempts to extinguish the fire cannot be continued without danger, or if they are clearly failing to keep the fire in check, the fire-fighter(s) should withdraw immediately and await the assistance of the fire brigade, having first checked that no-one is trapped. Any doors and windows that can be closed should be closed.

WARNING. Asphyxiant, irritant and toxic gases, smoke and fumes are a greater hazard to life than heat burns, especially in laboratories. Many plastic materials and cleansing fluids when heated give off highly noxious fumes. Carbon monoxide may be present when dealing with a fire in a confined space. Beware also of the danger of re-ignition, especially of Class B fires. Carbon dioxide or BCF vapours have little cooling effect and, if the blanket of inert vapour is displaced by air, re-ignition of the hot vapour may occur. In the case of foam or powder blankets, a similar hazard may also arise due to disturbance of the layer but this is less likely than with vapours.

Raising the alarm

This may be done verbally or by operating the installed system. In the case of a minor fire it may only be necessary to warn people in the immediate vicinity. The school fire alarm should only be sounded as a signal that the premises are to be evacuated, i.e. if the fire is spreading rapidly, if smoke is spreading in substantial amounts, or if stairways and other escape routes are threatened.

For a review of fire warning systems see D.E.S. Building Bulletin No. 7, p. 29.

Action on hearing the alarm

When the alarm sounds, everyone should WALK from the building via the nearest available exit and then go to the agreed assembly point. Most schools clearly indicate the fire exit routes from each of the rooms in the buildings.

At the assembly point, a teacher is responsible for ensuring that no-one in his charge is left in the building. It is not sufficient merely to call a roll, since this would not necessarily account for visitors, persons temporarily absent from the school or those pupils who had not yet arrived at the class from another lesson. It is up to every teacher to satisfy himself that none of his/her immediate colleagues, pupils or visitors are unaccounted for.

DO NOT USE LIFTS AFTER AN ALARM HAS SOUNDED

Lift shafts can act as chimneys or become smoke-logged. A power failure would result in the lift occupants being trapped.

GENERAL FIRE HAZARDS

Highly reactive chemicals, particularly strong oxidizing agents, should not be placed in waste bins where enough heat can be generated to bring about combustion. Fires due to a spontaneous combustion in waste bins are more common than is generally realized and, as they may occur during the night, are particularly dangerous.

Burns and scalds can be received from a variety of sources, e.g. burners that have blown back, non-luminous flames, hot glass, tripods, solvent fires, clothing set alight, overheated electrical equipment, electrical flash. ALL burns should receive medical or first aid treatment.

Burners should be in a physically stable position, protected from draughts and remote from flammable materials, especially organic solvents. Rubber tubing should be in good condition and protected from radiant heat. NEVER HEAT FLAMMABLE LIQUIDS WITH A NAKED FLAME.

Electrical and electronic apparatus can initiate fires due to the overheating of cable and components, or by arc or spark discharges. Electric heaters and soldering irons can be a source of danger. Overheating is generally caused by allowing a component to pass a higher current than that for which it is rated. Ensure that circuits are correctly fused. In more permanent installations cut-outs are to be preferred.

If an electric motor is stopped mechanically with the current flowing overheating will occur. Fires can result from the inadvertent obstruction of electric fan blades.

Static electricity can ignite flammable atmospheres. Charges can accumulate on metal drums from which non-conducting liquids, e.g. organic solvents, are being drawn. A spark of considerable energy can be generated. The danger can be avoided by earthing the bare metal surface of the drum.

Common hazards of organic solvents

A number of commonly used organic solvents possess characteristics which combine to produce a high degree of fire hazard:

(a) Low flashpoint

(Flashpoint is defined as the minimum temperature at which the vapour of a liquid gives rise to an explosive mixture with air.)

The flashpoints of some widely used organic liquids are:

	°C
95% ethanol (ethyl alcohol)	+13
methanol (methyl alcohol)	+10
benzene	−11
propanone (acetone)	−18
carbon disulphide	−30
ethanal (acetaldehyde)	−38
ethoxyethane (diethyl ether)	−45
40/60 petroleum ether	−51

Any of the last six solvents can produce a flammable atmosphere inside an ordinary refrigerator and should not be kept in one that is not guaranteed spark free.*

(b) Ease of ignition of vapour-air mixtures

The amount of electrical energy required to ignite vapour-air mixtures is very small (of the order of 200 micro-joules) and can be provided by static discharge, sparking of relay contacts or even the shorting of small dry batteries.

Many solvent vapours can be ignited by contact with surfaces below red heat. Carbon disulphide is especially dangerous, as its vapour can be ignited by contact with a steam radiator or a hot electric light bulb. Diethyl ether (ethoxyethane) has a self-ignition temperature of only 179 °C.

(c) High density vapours

High density vapours can creep along floors and benches for many feet providing a flammable or explosive train.

(d) Behaviour in confined spaces

When keeping solvent vapours in confined spaces, e.g. refrigerators, the following points should be borne in mind:

(i) the small percentage of vapour required to render an air/vapour mixture explosive: for ethanol, propanone, ethoxyethane and

* For further details of flashpoints, see *Flashpoints*, B.D.H. 1963.

carbon disulphide the required percentages are 2.3, 2.1, 1.2 and 1.0 respectively;

(ii) the small quantity of liquid which can produce enough vapour to form an explosive mixture even in a large enclosure. The evaporation of 5 cm^3 of benzene can produce an explosive atmosphere in a chamber 3 ft^3 (8×10^4 cm^3) in volume, e.g. a drying oven or refrigerator.

Spark-free refrigerators should be specified for laboratory use.

Refrigerators should be modified, when purchased, to remove spark sources from the cold chamber.

Flammable gases

The explosion hazards of flammable gases such as hydrogen, methane, propane etc. are similar to those of flammable vapours. Again, the wide limits of concentration for explosive gas/air mixtures and the ease of ignition are emphasized.

Particular care is required when acetylene is used, its ability to form shock sensitive acetylides with copper, silver and certain other metals enhancing the fire hazard.

Before introducing any gas cylinder into a laboratory or workshop the valve should be tested.

Flammable dusts and finely divided metals

Dust explosions are less likely to occur in laboratories than in industrial conditions but clouds of finely divided oxidizable materials, e.g. flour, coal-dust, sawdust, powdered metals, can be detonated in confined spaces, e.g. ventilation ducts.

Metals which are not readily ignited in massive form may become dangerously pyrophoric when finely powdered, e.g. iron freshly reduced from oxide, Raney nickel, etc.

Oxygen-enriched atmospheres

All fire hazards are considerably increased in oxygen-enriched atmospheres such as may surround Dewar vessels containing oxygen.

Liquid nitrogen is safer to use but can condense oxygen from the atmosphere; consequently, when liquid nitrogen cold traps have been in use continuously, care should be taken when the residual liquid evaporates from the Dewar. Where liquid air is used the nitrogen boils off first, leaving the oxygen behind.

ACTION

1 Make yourself THOROUGHLY familiar with the detailed fire orders exhibited in your particular work place. It is too late to start reading instructions when a fire has broken out.
2 At all times know the location of the nearest fire appliances, breathing sets and respirators APPROPRIATE to the materials with which you are working.

FIRE FIGHTING

Discretion is essential in deciding the lengths to which first-aid fire-fighting is carried. Portable fire-fighting equipment is not designed to cope with extensive fires and it is important that first-aid fire-fighting should cease and the location should be evacuated as soon as the fire threatens the means of escape or the building structure, or gets out of control. Although further action might reduce material losses, no such saving can compare in importance with human safety.

When fighting a fire remember:

1 Use the correct fire extinguisher. In a laboratory the wrong choice can turn a minor incident into a major disaster.
2 Do not use carbon tetrachloride (pyrene) or similar extinguishers where there is poor ventilation unless you are wearing breathing apparatus. The vapours are toxic.
3 Carbon dioxide extinguishers should be used with care. They can reduce the oxygen content of the atmosphere in a confined space to a dangerously low level.
4 A fire needs oxygen to burn but YOU need oxygen to breathe.
5 A respirator is only effective when fitted properly and only absorbs limited amounts of toxic vapours. It DOES NOT supply oxygen and is not suitable for use in high smoke areas.

5 First aid

Injuries may result from fires, explosions, the emission of toxic or irritant gases, falls, falling objects, machinery etc. The injuries may consist of any of the following main groups.

1 Eye injuries.
2 Respiratory effects due to the inhalation of:

    (a) asphyxiant gases;
    (b) corrosive or irritant gases;
    (c) toxic gases.

3 Burns and scalds.
4 Cuts and severe bleeding.
5 Shock.
6 Concussion.

    N.B. Any of these may involve radioactivity as a complicating hazard.

The philosophy of first-aid treatment

First-aid measures should aim at making the patient safe and comfortable and preventing his condition from worsening whilst awaiting the arrival of professional medical assistance.

The aim should be to achieve these objectives with the minimum of interference with the patient. It is most important that the patient be reassured and treated for shock. Severe bleeding or absence of breathing requires IMMEDIATE action.

Corrosive or toxic substances must be cleaned off as quickly as possible. DO NOT GIVE THE PATIENT ANYTHING TO DRINK. If a general anaesthetic is required later this can cause vomiting, with serious consequences.

Eye injuries

When the injury is due to a solid object skilled attention should be obtained immediately. If the injury is due to a splash of corrosive liquid the eye should be held open and washed with copious amounts of pure water. The pain suffered by the casualty may require physical force to be applied before this can be done.

N.B. Corrosive materials begin to damage the eye tissue after about 15 seconds.

All eye injuries should be seen by a Medical Officer.

Treatment of respiratory injury

Get the patient into the fresh air. If necessary apply artificial respiration. The patient should be seen by a medical practitioner as soon as possible and any known exposure to corrosive, irritant or toxic gases should be reported.

Mouth to mouth artificial respiration

REMEMBER: START ARTIFICIAL RESPIRATION AS QUICKLY AS POSSIBLE— THE FIRST MINUTES ARE VITAL

1 Pull the victim clear of immediate danger of further injury.

N.B. If an electric shock is the cause of unconsciousness either switch off the current or use an insulating material to pull the victim away from the conductor.

2 Lay the victim on his back and remove any obstructions from the mouth and throat, e.g. loose dentures, plant material ingested during drowning.

3 Put one hand under the neck and the other on the forehead of the patient and tilt the head right back, raising the chin up. This prevents the tongue blocking the air passage in the throat.

4 Seal the patient's nostrils either by pinching with the fingers or by resting the cheek against the nostrils.

5 Breathe in deeply, seal your lips round the patient's mouth and blow into his lungs until they are filled, watching the chest rise.

6 Remove your mouth and watch the chest of the patient fall, at the same time taking another breath.

7 Repeat the process.

8 If for any reason, e.g. injury, the rescuer cannot seal his mouth over the patient's mouth, close the patient's mouth and blow through the nose of the patient, using the same technique as for the mouth-to-mouth resuscitation.

If necessary artificial respiration should be carried out for at least an hour.

REMEMBER. Permanent damage to the brain results if it is deprived of oxygen for more than four minutes.

The patient should be kept under medical observation for 24 hours after resuscitation.

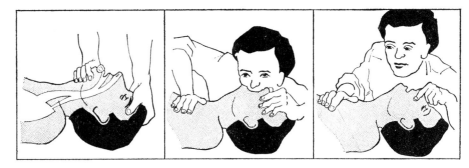

N.B. Compressed air breathing apparatus, if available, may be used as a source of fresh air if the patient cannot be moved quickly, e.g. because of back injury.

Respiratory protection

Ordinary respirators are of limited use for the following reasons:

(i) in order to be effective they must be carefully fitted to ensure that the air breathed passes through the canister and not round the sides of the face-piece;

(ii) they only protect against low concentrations of gas (about 1% by volume of toxic gas in air);

(iii) respirators do not provide oxygen and therefore are of no value in an oxygen depleted area;

(iv) there is no canister which gives protection against all known toxic gases.

When dealing with laboratory incidents the use of compressed air breathing apparatus is recommended.

Burns

Chemical burns

Wash with copious amounts of water. If damage to the skin has resulted a suitable dressing should be applied by a qualified person.

Heat burns

Tissue damage due to burns results firstly, from direct contact with the external source of heat and, secondly, from conduction of heat from the tissue damaged by the external heat source to the neighbouring tissue. It is this secondary effect which causes damage to the deeper tissues.

Rapid cooling of the burn can greatly restrict the secondary effects and so limit the severity of the burn.

Burn injuries are accompanied by loss of fluid (plasma) from the blood into the tissues (causing swelling) and by oozing from the wound, the injured area rapidly becoming red, swollen, blistered and painful. Shock may be expected related to the severity of the burn.

If the clothing is on fire it is imperative that the victim gets, or is put, into a horizontal position immediately, to limit the spread of injury. Extinguish the flames by rolling the victim in a blanket or by other suitable action. Any charred material, which will be sterile, should be left *in situ* by the First Aider.

Treatment should aim at:

(a) reducing the effects of heat and the alleviation of pain;
(b) reducing discomfort and swelling;
(c) limiting the risk of contamination and infection of the wound;
(d) ensuring that the patient takes sufficient fluid;
(e) reassuring the patient and lessening the shock.

Management of burns:

(i) Cool the injury as rapidly as possible by immersion in cold water, irrigating with running cold water or by the application of ice-packs.
(ii) After thorough cooling apply a dry, sterile dressing to the wound.
(iii) Remove promptly anything of a constricting nature, e.g. rings, bangles, belts, boots.

DO NOT apply any lotions, ointments or oil dressings.
DO NOT prick blisters.

The following information is provided to enable the severity of an injury to be judged.

If more than 10% of the body surface is damaged the injury should be regarded as VERY SEVERE and it is of the utmost urgency to get the patient to hospital.

In order to estimate the area affected the rule of nines may be taken as a rough guide.

Head	1/9 of body surface (approx. 11%)	
Arm	1/9	,,
Leg	2/9	,,
Front of trunk	1/9	,,
Back of trunk	1/9	,,

The hand, when laid flat with the fingers together, covers approximately 1% of the body surface; the face is approximately 3% of the body surface.

High radio-frequency burns

Although with radio-frequencies there is no electric shock as normally understood, the burn arising from this cause must not be dismissed as of no account. The outward appearance of blisters may be slight but the damage is invariably deep-seated and always liable to be slow-healing and extremely painful. Therefore all cases of radio-frequency burns, however apparently slight, must be reported and must receive medical attention.

Treatment of severe bleeding

Cuts and severe bleeding

These should be washed thoroughly with water and a sterile dressing applied. Do not apply antiseptics.

When the cut was caused by a rough dirty object, e.g. a rusty nail, it is advisable to report to a medical officer for an anti-tetanus injection or toxoid boost.

Pressure points and severe arterial bleeding

Severe bleeding due to a severed artery must be controlled as quickly as possible.

Bleeding from an artery is recognized by the flow being bright red and in spurts. In large wounds the spurts of blood will be from the end of the wound nearest the heart.

Bleeding may be restricted by applying pressure at an appropriate point on an artery between the heart and the wound. The artery must be compressed onto the underlying bone. The principal pressure points are shown on the diagram and may be located by feeling for the pulse at the appropriate point. The flow of blood is stopped by applying firm pressure to the artery. In the case of the pressure point in the groin it is necessary to place both thumbs over the artery and to press very hard.

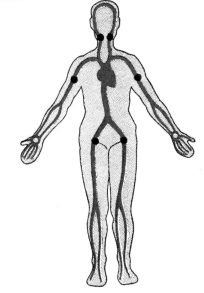

Concussion

When a blow on the head has been sustained the patient should be seen by a qualified first-aid worker. If there is any possibility of concussion having been suffered a medical officer should be consulted. Do not allow the patient to take the decision—his sense of judgement may have been affected if the blow was severe.

Treatment of shock

Shock is a state of collapse which is fatal if not brought under control and which may result from physical or emotional injury. It is a weakening of the blood circulation caused by either severe loss of blood or the pooling of blood in the abdominal region resulting in an inadequate supply to the brain and other vital centres.

Symptoms may include: faintness, giddiness, complaint of blurred vision, collapse, pallor, clammy or cold skin or the breaking into a sweat, and anxiety.

Treatment. The patient should be laid down and if possible the feet raised higher than the head.

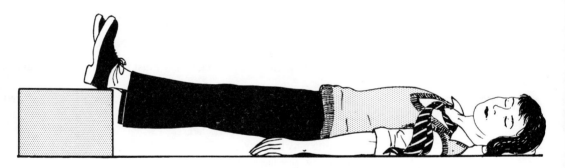

Reassure the patient and allay his anxiety. Make the patient comfortable and carry out any other necessary treatment, but do not move the patient unnecessarily. Get the patient to hospital as quickly as possible—a blood transfusion may be necessary.

DO NOT OVERHEAT A SHOCKED PATIENT. This causes the superficial blood vessels to increase their capacity at the expense of the circulation. The patient may be protected by a blanket.

First-aid kits

First-aid kits must be provided in adequate numbers and kept in places accessible to teachers, technical staff and pupils. Responsibility for maintaining the stock of first-aid kits must be clearly defined. Pupils must be made aware of the location and contents of first-aid kits and should be taught how to use them.

The contents of a first-aid kit should be as simple as possible and the following are suggested.

1 pair blunt-ended scissors
Assorted bandages
Triangular bandage (sling)
Adhesive plaster and dressings
Sterilized cotton wool
Sterilized gauze
Mild antiseptic solution
Safety pins
Small forceps

If necessary, advice on the contents of a first-aid kit may be obtained from the school Medical Officer.

6 The teacher and the law

On appointment to a school, a teacher normally signs a written contract defining the agreement between himself and the employing authority. Note that the contract may be taken to include any further particulars supplied when the post was advertised or in a letter of appointment. In maintained schools every full-time teacher must be supplied with a copy of his contract, together with access to any regulations referred to therein.

If you are yourself injured in the course of your science teaching duties, it is not possible for you to obtain damages from your employer unless he can be shown to be guilty of negligence. It follows that if you wish to insure yourself against such injury and the loss of any income etc. such insurance must be arranged at your expense. However, it is important that you take the initiative in reporting, preferably in writing, any hazards which it is the responsibility of the employer to rectify, e.g. faulty fume cupboards, defective gas, water or electricity outlets. The date of any such report should be noted.

Accidents involving pupils

Similar considerations apply to accidents involving pupils. You are not liable for the results of an accident to a pupil in your charge unless it is established that you have, in some way, been negligent. In this case, negligence can be taken to mean failure to act as would a reasonable parent with expert knowledge. Hence it is important that the necessary precautions should be observed and that pupils be asked to undertake only those experiments commensurate with their age, ability and experience. Pupils must have, and understand, copies of the laboratory rules. They must also be given *explicit* warning of any hazard associated with a particular experiment, technique or material. Your duty as a teacher is to design the teaching-learning situation in such a way as to remove, or at least minimize, such hazards.

In the event of an accident to pupils it is important to seek medical opinion unless you are *in no doubt* that this is unnecessary. Failure to summon medical attention in such a situation could constitute negligence. Similarly it is important that you make a *factual* report on the accident as soon as it is reasonable to do so after an accident. Many local authorities will have a standard procedure to be followed in such cases. Remember that an accident is an uncontrolled situation in which you will be emotionally, if not physically, involved: some time for reflection and the consultation of any witnesses, e.g. a laboratory technician, is therefore desirable before you formally submit your account of an accident.

You should also consider seeking expert legal advice, e.g. that normally offered by one of the professional associations.

If a parent decides to sue the 'employing authority' for damages, he may do so singly against any individual authority (e.g. the L.E.A., or the headmaster or teacher(s) involved) or jointly against any combination. Any damages may be apportioned between those responsible for the negligent act(s).

When a pupil is injured at school, you may offer or be asked to take the injured pupil home or to hospital. If your motor vehicle insurance is restricted in its coverage to social, domestic or pleasure purposes, it could constitute an offence to transport a pupil in this way. However, most Local Authorities have effected suitable Motor Contingent Liability Policies which indemnify teachers in respect of their legal liability for accidents to third parties arising from the use of a car in direct connection with out-of-school activities and insofar as their own insurance arrangements are inadequate for the purpose. It is also a relatively inexpensive undertaking to modify an individual motor insurance policy to provide the necessary cover. Science teachers, like their colleagues, should therefore establish the legal position so far as such insurance is concerned, *before* an emergency or other situation arises.

Legal liabilities of student teachers

The position of a student teacher undertaking teaching practice in a maintained school differs from that of other teachers in the school in that the student teacher is not an employee of the Local Education Authority. An L.E.A. provides indemnity for its employees by means of a Public Liability Insurance policy which normally relates to matters arising from the law of negligence, e.g. injury to a pupil or conduct causing injury to a third party. Despite the fact that student teachers have no written contract of service with an employing authority, it is likely that no distinction will be made between an employee and a student teacher as far as the protection offered by Public Liability Insurance is concerned. Similarly, if a student teacher suffered injury from a pupil or a third party while acting in the normal course of his work, he would normally receive the same degree of insurance protection as an L.E.A. employee.

The legal position of student teachers undertaking teaching practice in independent schools may differ somewhat from that described above. However, it is probable that the governors of non-maintained schools will have taken out insurance policies designed to offer cover similar to that provided by L.E.A. Public Liability Insurance.

It should be noted that Administrative Memorandum 2/76 includes a number of provisions for student teachers using ionizing radiations on teaching practice. For a summary of these provisions see page 31.

Out-of-school activities

As a science teacher your work with pupils may well take you outside the school premises, e.g. on field trips or science society visits. It is important that any such activities are formally regarded as official school functions by your employer. Some L.E.A.s publish a list of approved out-of-school activities which effectively, if not legally, provides an indemnity against any claim for damages made on behalf of a pupil while he is on such an approved course or engaged in a listed activity. In some cases it is reasonable to ask parents to sign an indemnity against any claim made on behalf of their child in the charge of a teacher conducting an out-of-school activity.* Such indemnities are only as valid as the ability of the signatory to pay and should be sought only after appropriate advice has been taken.

Such advice is usually available from one of the professional associations. Membership of such an association normally provides for legal and financial assistance in meeting claims for damages. Those teachers who are not members of a professional association would be wise to insure themselves privately. Note that an insurance policy is unlikely to be declared inoperative because a claim is based on negligence, unless, for example, such negligence could be reasonably construed as a *deliberate* neglect of duty.

Experimental work controlled by law

There are a number of Acts of Parliament and Orders in Council which govern the work of any teacher in a school and some of these have particular relevance to the science teacher. In addition there may be local authority regulations. The following should be noted:

1 Industrial methylated spirit (95% ethanol-water and 5% naphtha) and duty free spirit (ethanol-water) cannot be obtained without a

---

* It is possible that an L.E.A.'s own insurance already provides adequate cover for recognized out-of-school activities. Unnecessary indemnities should be avoided.

requisition order from the local office of the Customs and Excise department. It is necessary to give an undertaking that the spirit will be securely stored, used exclusively for science teaching and be accounted for in a return made of the amount used for teaching purposes. If it is required to purify industrial methylated or duty free spirit, special permission must be obtained. Note that mineralized methylated spirit may be easily purchased although it is, of course, of very limited use in schools.

2 The making of explosive mixtures is governed by the Explosives Act of 1875 which provides that it is unlawful to make explosives without permission under licence from the Home Secretary.

Pupils should not be shown how to make fireworks or rocket fuels. The making of fireworks by pupils is annually responsible for a number of serious accidents. Certain procedures, e.g. the mixing of phosphorus or sulphur with potassium chlorate(V), are forbidden by law.

Some preparations and reactions are unnecessary in school science teaching, e.g. nitrogen tri-iodide, explosion of acetylene (ethyne) and oxygen, or of hydrogen and chlorine, preparation of oxides of chlorine etc. For a fuller list see the D.E.S. *Safety in Science Laboratories*, Chapter 12.

It is your duty as a science teacher to indicate the hazardous nature of many materials and to indicate to pupils how far-reaching may be the consequences of an accident with explosives.

Note that some reactions need special care but, with appropriate precautions, may be reasonably and safely demonstrated in a school. For a list of such reactions see again D.E.S. *Safety in Science Laboratories*, Chapter 12.

3 Although access to poisonous chemicals by pupils is a necessary part of work in a school, adequate precautions to secure and monitor the stock are essential. The storage and handling of potentially dangerous substances, e.g. gas cylinders, flammable liquids, are governed by several Acts of Parliament which were not drawn up with schools particularly in mind. Other regulations on storage may be laid down by the L.E.A. and such regulations are likely to be based on these Acts and associated Orders in Council. Clearly the contents of such regulations should be consulted by the teacher.

The regulations relating to the storage and use of radioactive materials (see D.E.S. Administrative Memorandum 2/76 and S.E.D. Circulars 689, 852 and 882) and of highly flammable liquids are of particular importance. The Highly Flammable and Liquefied Petroleum Gases Regulations, 1972, (No. 917) came into effect on 21 June 1973. A 'Highly Flammable Liquid' (HFL) is defined as 'any liquid, liquid solution, emulsion or suspension which, when tested in a specified manner . . . gives off a flammable vapour at a temperature of less than 32 °C and supports combustion'.

Quantities up to 50 litres of highly flammable liquids may be kept in a preparation room, *provided* that they are stored in a suitably placed cupboard or bin made of fire-resisting material and fitted with retention sills to contain any spillage. Larger quantities must be kept in a separate structure away from the science laboratories. No more than 500 cm³ of any one highly flammable liquid should be kept on any shelf in a school laboratory.

All storerooms, cupboards, bins and other containers, used for storing highly flammable liquids must be clearly labelled with the words HIGHLY FLAMMABLE or FLASHPOINT BELOW 32 °C.

Note also that there are stringent regulations governing the disposal of waste materials (see page 18) and the transport of radioactive, toxic, flammable or otherwise hazardous substances. A teacher's domestic motor insurance policy could be rendered inoperative if he used his car to transport apparatus and/or chemicals from one site to another.

4 Work with radioactive substances and X-rays is rigidly controlled in schools. The position has been outlined earlier. For details see Administrative Memorandum 2/76.

5 An increasingly large number and variety of animals are being used in the teaching of school science. The work which can be done with live animals is strictly controlled by the law. The position is reviewed in some detail in the A.S.E. publication, *Biology Teaching in School Involving Experiments or Demonstration with Animals or with Pupils*.

If there is any doubt about the interpretation or application of the appropriate legislation as far as any school experiment involving animals is concerned, the advice of the Home Office Inspectorate should be sought. Teachers responsible for work with any living organism are strongly urged to consult the publications referred to on page 40.

6 The Conservation of Wild Creatures and Wild Plants Act 1975, makes it an offence to uproot any wild plant without the permission of the landowner. A number of species of plants and of animals are under additional legislative protection and must not be collected in any circumstances. Specimens collected in the field should not include species known to be rare, either locally or nationally. If there is any doubt over a particular specimen, it should be identified *before* a decision is reached as to whether it

should be collected. For advice on the collection and preservation of plant material, teachers are referred to the various publications of the British Museum (Natural History) in the series *Instructions for Collectors*.

7 In certain teaching situations, e.g. rural science where pupils may be working on a farm, other activities will be controlled by specialist regulations. For example, the Farm Safety Regulations do not allow children under 13 to ride on a tractor, on farm implements or on trailers (except the floor of the trailer).

The Health and Safety at Work Act

The Health and Safety at Work etc. Act, 1974, applies to all persons at work, except domestic workers in private households, and is an enabling measure, superimposed upon existing health and safety legislation. The Act provides for the gradual replacement of existing health and safety requirements by revised and updated provisions. Existing Statutory Regulations under previous legislation remain in force until they are replaced by alternative regulations and codes of practice under the new Act. The Act is comprehensive in scope and its detailed implications for schools and other educational establishments are still being elaborated.

The Act became applicable to schools and colleges on 1 April 1975. Responsibility for administering the Act lies with the Health and Safety Commission and its Executive which appoints inspectors to carry out its enforcement functions. The inspectors have power to issue improvement or prohibition notices, in order to require action to remedy a contravention, or stop an activity which causes risk of serious personal injury. Under the Commission's guidance, local authorities will enforce the legislation in 'non-industrial' areas of employment and regulations are to be issued after appropriate consultation.

The following points are of particular importance to school science teachers.

1 The Act requires all employers to prepare and, where necessary, to revise written statements setting out their *policy* for the health and safety of employees and the procedures for effecting that policy.

2 The Act requires that all reasonably practical steps be taken to train employees in health and safety issues. This provision emphasizes the need to ensure that technicians, as well as teachers are properly trained in safety matters.

3 Designers, manufacturers, importers (suppliers of articles or substances) for use in schools or colleges must ensure that, so far as is reasonably practicable, they are safe when properly used.

This means that an article must be tested for safety in use and that details must be given of any conditions of use regarding its safety.

4 Teachers have a duty under the Act to take reasonable care to avoid injury to themselves or to others by their teaching activities, and to cooperate with employers and others in meeting statutory requirements. The Act also requires employees not to interfere with or misuse anything provided to protect their health, safety or welfare in compliance with the Act. This provision emphasizes the importance of adequate supervision of laboratories at all times and of conducting a systematic check on laboratory safety on a daily, weekly, termly and annual basis. For a suggested 'Safety Check List' see *Education in Science*, 1975, 75, pp. 18–19 and D.E.S., *Safety in Science Laboratories*, 1978, Chapter 13.

5 Section 37 of the Act makes it clear that if an offence against the Act is committed by a corporate body, not only the corporation but also the individual(s) who have been responsible by consent, neglect, connivance etc. may be subject to legal action.

6 An employer is required 'to give to persons (not being his employees) who may be affected by the way in which he conducts his undertaking, the prescribed information about such aspects of the way he conducts his undertaking as might affect their health or safety'. This sub-section of the Act could be considered as covering risks to pupils in schools and students in colleges and appropriate safety training should be provided.

7 The Health and Safety Commission, after appropriate consultation, will issue Regulations and approved codes of practice. These codes of practice will have a special legal status as they will not be statutory requirements but may be used in criminal proceedings as evidence that a statutory requirement has been contravened.

8 The Act provides for recognized Trades Unions to appoint safety representatives from among the employees and requires an employer, if requested by the safety representatives, to appoint a safety committee.

The Health and Safety Act places an obligation on both teachers and administrators to develop and publicize appropriate safety education procedures. Some L.E.A.s already issue science teachers with a loose-leaf Safety Manual, produced by a Safety Committee charged with producing instructions and recommendations and with circulating these to appropriate individuals and organizations within the Authority. It is possible that this or a similar practice will become more widespread and be extended to all local authority employees.

Immediate responsibility for disseminating information about safety matters within a school science department is likely to lie with the Head of department. Such a person should ensure that:

(i)   all members of the department, including technicians, student-teachers and newly appointed staff, are made fully aware of the school/L.E.A. safety policy and procedures;

(ii) all members of the department are made aware of any changes in safety policy or procedure;

(iii) proper procedures exist for checking the safety of laboratory fixtures, equipment and stores and that the relevant checks are conducted on a daily, weekly, termly or annual basis as appropriate;

(iv) first-aid boxes, fire blankets and extinguishers, sand buckets, spectacles or goggles and other items of safety equipment are checked regularly and any deficiencies made good;

(v)   all accidents, however minor, are reported and recorded in accordance with the required procedure;

(vi) the attention of the appropriate authorities (Headmaster, L.E.A. etc.) is drawn to any significant new hazards arising from changes in the science taught within the school (e.g. radioactivity);

(vii) the safety of all aspects of science teaching within the school is kept under review, referring such matters as he feels to be outside his competence to the appropriate Local Authority Adviser in the first instance.

Further information about the operation of the Health and Safety at Work etc. Act, 1974, may be obtained from the local offices of the Health and Safety Executive, from the pamphlets produced by the Health and Safety Commission or from the following publications:

Broadhurst, V. A., *The Health and Safety at Work Act in Practice*, Heyden, 1978.

Curson, C., *Health and Safety at Work in the Public Services*, Councils and Education Press, 1978.

D.E.S. *Health and Safety at Work etc. 1974*, Circular 11/74 (226/74, Welsh Office).

T.U.C. *Health and Safety at Work–A T.U.C. Guide* 1975.

Note also the following:

'Professional Judgement and Safety in Science Teaching' *Education in Science*, 1976, 68, pp. 20–21 and 1977, 71, p. 22.

'Science Teachers and the Health and Safety Act', *Education in Chemistry*, 1975, **12**, 6, pp. 167–168.

Select Bibliography

General

Archenhold, W. F., Jenkins, E. W., Wood-Robinson, C., *School Science Laboratories: a handbook of design, management and organization*, Murray, 1978.

Association for Science Education, *Safeguards in the School Laboratory*, A.S.E., 1976.

Bretherick, L., *Handbook of Reactive Chemical Hazards*, Butterworths, 1979.

British Standards Institution.
Recommendations for Health and Safety in Workshops of Schools and colleges, BS 4163, 1975.
Classification of Fires, BS:EN 1972.

Chemical Society, *Code of Practice for Chemistry Laboratories*, 1975.

Christensen, H. E. *et al* (eds.), *Registry of Toxic Effects of Chemical Substances*, U.S.A. Dept. of Health, Education and Welfare.

C.L.E.A.P.S.E.
Electrical Safety for the Users of School Laboratories, C.L.E.A.P.S.E./ A.S.E., 1978.
Hazcards, 1978 (available only in L.E.A.s which are members of C.L.E.A.P.S.E.)

Department of Education and Science, *Administrative Memoranda*.
2/65 'Poisonous substances in pencils and other allied materials used in schools'.
17/67 'National water safety campaign'.
20/67 'Inhalation of Asbestos Dust'.
3/70 'Avoidance of Carcinogenic Aromatic Amines in Schools and other Educational Establishments'.
7/70 'The Use of Lasers in Schools'.
11/73 'Constructional standards for maintained and direct grant building in England and Wales (Amendment 4/74)'.
2/76 'The Use of Ionizing Radiations in Educational Establishments' and the associated 'Notes for Guidance'.
6/76 'The Laboratory Use of Dangerous Pathogens'.
7/76 'The Use of Asbestos in Educational Establishments (Welsh Office 4/76)'.

Department of Education and Science, *Circulars and Letters*.
7/74 'Work Experience'.
11/74 'Health and Safety at Work, etc. Act, 1974'.
FECL 30/65 'Training in Safety'.
FECL 1/70 'Safety Training in Colleges of Further Education'.
M30/33/03 'Poisonous substances in materials used in schools (Dec. 1972)'.

M72/0143 'Use of benzene in schools and other educational establishments (April, 1974)'.

T42/47/041 'High pressure oxygen (manifold) systems (February 1975)'.

Department of Education and Science *Safety Series*.

No. 2 *Safety in Science Laboratories*, H.M.S.O., 1978.

No. 3 *Safety in Practical Departments*, H.M.S.O., 1977.

No. 5 *Safety in Further Education*, H.M.S.O., 1976.

No. 6 *Safety at School: General Advice*, H.M.S.O., 1979.

Department of Employment, *Code of Practice for reducing the exposure of employed persons to noise*, 1972.

Ellis, J. G., Riches, N. J., *Safety and Laboratory Practice*, Macmillan, 1978.

Gaston, P. J., *The Care, Handling and Disposal of Dangerous Chemicals*, Northern Publishers, (Aberdeen) Ltd, 1965.

Green, M. E., Turk, A., *Safety in Working with Chemicals*, Macmillan, 1978.

Guy, K., *Laboratory Organization and Administration*, Macmillan, 1973.

Health and Safety Executive, *Threshold Limit Values*, published annually.

Hughes, D., *Hazards of Occupational Exposure to Ultra-violet Radiation*, University of Leeds, 1978.

Laporte Chemicals, *Code of Practice for the Storage of Organic Peroxides*, Warrington, Lancs.

Muir, G. D., (ed.) *Hazards in the Chemical Laboratory*, Chemical Society, 1977.

Royal Society/Institute of Biology, *Dissections of Animals in Schools*, a report by the Biological Education Committee, 1976.

Scottish Education Department, *Circulars*.

No. 689 (1968), *Ionizing Radiations in Schools, Colleges of Education and Further Education Establishments*.

No. 766 (1970), *Use of Lasers in Schools, Colleges of Education and Further Education Establishments*.

No. 825 (1972), *The Use of Carcinogenic Substances in Educational Establishments*.

No. 852 (1973), *The Temporary Use of Ionizing Radiation in Schools, Colleges of Education and Further Education Establishments for Demonstrations by Visiting Lecturers or Student Teachers in Training*.

No. 882 (1973), *Special Precautions for the Safe Handling of Radium 226 Closed Sources of an Approved type for Use in Schools, Colleges of Education and Further Education Establishments*.

Scottish Education Department, *Memoranda*.

39/66 *The Hazards of Experimenting with Explosives*.

6/68 *Inhalation of Asbestos Dust*, (under review).

8/74 *High Pressure Oxygen (Manifold) Systems*.

Scottish Schools Science Equipment Research Centre, *Hazardous Chemicals, A Manual for Schools and Colleges*, Oliver and Boyd, 1979.

Steere, N. V., *Safety in the Chemical Laboratory*, Pennsylvania, 1971.

University of Leeds, *Safety Handbook*, 3rd edition, 1980.

Teachers and the law

Barrell, G. R., *Legal Cases for Teachers*, Methuen, 1970.

Broadhurst, V. A., *The Health and Safety at Work Act in Practice*, Heyden, 1978.

Cooke, A. J. D., *A Guide to Laboratory Law*, Butterworths, 1976.
Curson, C., *Health and safety at work in the public services*, Councils and Education Press, 1978.
Department of Education and Science, *Health and Safety at Work, etc. Act*, Circular 11/74 (226/74 Welsh Office).
Elgin, H., *The Law and the Teacher*, Ward Lock, 1967.
Everton, Ann R., *Fire and the Law*, Butterworth, 1972.
Health and Safety Executive, *Health and Safety: The Safety Representatives and Safety Committees Regulations*, S.I. No. 500, 1977.
Robinson, F. A., Amies, F. A., *Chemists and the Law*, Spon, 1967.
T.U.C., *Health and Safety at Work: a T.U.C. Guide*, 1975.

Work with living organisms, including microbiology

A.S.E., *Biology Teaching in Schools Involving Experiments or Demonstrations with Animals or with Pupils*, 1972.
Bainbridge, B. W., 'Microbiology in Schools Advisory Committee (MISAC)', *J. Biol. Ed.*, 1972, **6**, pp. 207–210.
Dade, H. A., Gunnell, J., *Classwork with Fungi*, Commonwealth Mycological Institute, 1969.
Department of Education and Science.
    Keeping Animals in Schools: a Handbook for Teachers, H.M.S.O., 1971.
    The use of micro-organisms in schools, Education Pamphlet No. 61, H.M.S.O., 1977.
Holt, G., 'Practical tips for the safe-handling of micro-organisms in schools', *School Science Review*, 1974, 195, **56**, pp. 248–252.
Ministry of Agriculture, Fisheries and Food, *British Poisonous Plants*, Bulletin No. 161, H.M.S.O., 1968.
North, P., *Poisonous Plants and Fungi*, Blandford Press, 1967.
Schools Council, *Recommended practice for schools relating to the use of living organisms and material of living origin*, E.U.P., 1974.
Schools Council Educational Use of Living Organisms Project;
    The Educational Use of Living Organisms: a source book,
    Animal Accommodation for Schools, E.U.P., 1974.
    Micro-organisms, Hodder and Stoughton, 1974.
    Organisms for Genetics, Hodder and Stoughton, 1974.
    Plants, Hodder and Stoughton, 1977.
    Small Mammals, E.U.P., 1974.
Seamer, J. (ed.), *Safety in the Animal House*, Lab. Animals Ltd., 1972.
Shapton, D. A., Board, R. G. (eds.), *Safety in Microbiology*, Academic Press, 1972.
U.F.A.W.
    Handbook on the Care and Management of Laboratory Animals, 1972.
    Humane Killing of Animals, 1968.

Field work

British Mountaineering Council, *Mountain Code* and *Exposure*, 1968.
Campbell, I., *Law of Footpaths*, Commons, Open Spaces and Footpaths, Preservation Society, 1968.
Central Council of Physical Recreation, *Safety on Mountains*, 1968.

Department of Education and Science, *Camping*, Education Pamphlet No. 58, H.M.S.O., 1971.

Department of Education and Science, *Safety in Outdoor Pursuits*, Safety Series No. 1, H.M.S.O., 1977.

Schools Council, *Out and about, A teacher's guide to safety on educational visits*, Evans/Methuen Educational, 1972.

Visual aids and other teaching materials

Deeson, E., Armstrong, A., *Safety in the Science Laboratory*, Diana Wyllie Ltd, a filmstrip/slide set with lecture notes and commentary.

Department of Education and Science, *In the Movies it doesn't hurt*, a film for pupils on safety in school laboratories, 1975.

Educational Use of Living Organisms Project: Small Mammals, a set of posters and slides to complement the book with this title, E.U.P., 1974.

Fire Protection Association, *Education in Fire*, some suggestions for bringing the subject of fire into the ordinary school syllabus. Available from Aldermary House, Queen St, W1.

Pharmaceutical Society of Great Britain, *Common Poisonous Plants and Fungi*, a set of 40 transparencies in colour (35 mm).

Philip Harris Ltd, *Safety Matters*, a resource pack for training students in laboratory safety.

Royal Society for the Prevention of Accidents, Wallcharts on *Poisonous Fungi* and *These Fruits are Dangerous*.

Royal Society for the Prevention of Accidents, pads of sketches of laboratory situations in which pupils are asked to '*spot the hazard*'.

Science Teacher Education Project, *Laboratory Safety Hazards*, The Slide Centre; a set of 'spot the hazard' coloured transparencies.

For other safety materials produced by the Project see the relevant sections of *Activities and Experiences: a source book for tutors*, McGraw Hill, 1974.

Appendix A

HUMAN BLOOD SAMPLING: RECOMMENDED PROCEDURES

1 The approval of the School Medical Officer must be obtained for a sterile procedure (e.g. Section 1 below). It is best if permission is obtained by a Local Education Authority for all its schools.

2 Teachers must ensure that the pupils understand fully the precautions to be taken and the possible consequences of not taking them. This is valuable as a contribution to general knowledge as well as essential for the blood sampling to be safe.

3 There must be no pressure on a pupil to give a sample. Teachers should make it clear by their attitude that it is perfectly normal for some pupils not to want to have a sample taken and not to want to take any part in the practical work involved. If this is done well, it is likely that such pupils will gradually become involved in the work. Pupils should be allowed to change their minds either way.

4 Parental permission must be obtained, well in advance. A suitable form is given in Section 2 of this Appendix.

5 We would recommend that the teacher take the samples. If the pupils take their own samples, it is much harder for the teacher to ensure that the correct sterile procedure is followed by them all. (See Section 1). Also, children who are quite willing and eager for samples to be taken often find it impossible to do it themselves. We recommend that teachers ask pupils to sign the relevant part of the form in Section 2, or some similar statement.

6 Blood should be taken with a sterile lancet from the back of pupil's finger, near the nail, using a new lancet for each pupil. We do not recommend that blood be taken from a finger tip because of the risk of subsequent infection nor from the ear lobe because of danger if a pupil jerks his head. The best point is 5 to 10 mm from the lower corner of the nail. It is easier to insert the lancet if the finger has been crooked at the top joint.

7 Teachers must supervise the issue, use and subsequent disposal of the lancets extremely carefully.

8 The sterile procedure approved by the School Medical Officer (e.g. Section 1) should be adhered to.

SECTION 1

Suggested sterile procedure

Before the lesson

1 Slides or any other glassware which might possibly come into contact with the site from which a blood sample is taken should be sterilized by autoclaving to 103.5 kilopascal (103.5 kN m^{-2}, 15 lbf in^{-2}, 121 °C) or by heating dry for 3 hours at 170 °C.

2 An aqueous solution of sodium chlorate(I) (sodium hypochlorite) should be freshly prepared from a concentrated sodium chlorate(I) (sodium hypochlorite) solution such as Milton, Chloros or BDH sodium hypochlorite solution (10–14% w/v available chlorine). 10cm^3 of one of these should be added for every 1 dm^3 (litre) of solution. Such a solution should have a minimum concentration of free chlorine of 200 mg dm^{-3} (or ppm w/v); this concentration will turn starch iodide paper dark blue.

During the lesson

3 Because of the risk of contamination through broken skin, the participation in this practical work of anyone with any sort of open wound, particularly on or near the face or hands, should be strictly limited; depending on the nature and position of the wound, the pupil may need to be excluded from the work altogether.

4 Pupils and teacher must thoroughly wash both hands using soap and water. Those giving blood samples must pay particular attention to washing the site chosen for the sampling. Dry hands using disposable towels. If the teacher is taking the samples, he must wash and dry his hands before taking each sample.

5 Using a cotton wool swab, wipe the chosen site with 70% alcohol (70% v/v, propan-2-ol (*iso*-propanol) or ethanol)* and allow it to dry.

6 Remove a new sterile disposable lancet from its packet immediately prior to its use. Do not allow the sharp end to touch anything.

7 Puncture the skin in the chosen site using the lancet and immediately put it in a strong sealable container. LANCETS MUST BE USED ONCE ONLY.

8 Collect the blood by letting a drop or two fall into a sterile tube or on to a sterile slide. (See 1) There must be no contact between the area of the pinprick and any apparatus unless the apparatus has been sterilized.

9 Using a fresh cotton wool swab, wipe the site again with 70%

alcohol (70% v/v propan-2-ol (*iso*-propanol) or ethanol).* Apply slight pressure with the swab if necessary to stop the blood flow. Put the swabs in the container with the lancets.

10 Any blood spilt on the bench etc., must be wiped up immediately using the freshly prepared aqueous solution of sodium chlorate(I) (sodium hypochlorite). (See 2) Hold the swab with forceps or wear rubber or plastic gloves.

11 The greatest care must be taken to avoid contamination of the skin with blood from another person. If this should occur, however, the contaminated area must be disinfected immediately with the freshly prepared aqueous solution of sodium chlorate(I) (sodium hypochlorite), diluted with water to 10 times its volume, and then washed thoroughly with soap and water.

12 At the end of the practical, wash both hands using soap and water and dry them thoroughly using only disposable towels.

After the lesson

13 The container with the lancets and swabs should be sealed and autoclaved. Alternatively, immerse the swabs and used lancets in the freshly prepared aqueous solution of sodium chlorate(I) (sodium hypochlorite) and leave overnight. Then dispose of the container so that there is no danger of anyone coming into contact with the contaminated items.

14 All tubes, slides and other equipment contaminated with blood should be soaked in the freshly prepared aqueous solution of sodium chlorate(I) (sodium hypochlorite) overnight before being washed in the normal way. Rubber or plastic gloves should be worn.

* Or any other antiseptic approved by the School Medical Officer. Sterile injection swabs, impregnated with antiseptic, are obtainable from suppliers.

SECTION 2

Dear Parent,

During the next few weeks, we shall be studying blood during science lessons. Children usually find it very interesting to look at samples of their own blood under a microscope and to carry out other investigations with it.

This letter is to ask your permission for a sample of blood to be taken from your child. Please note that:

1 only a drop or two will be taken from a prick in a finger;
2 the School Medical Officer has approved the sterile procedure we will use;
3 the sample will be taken only if your child wants it to be done and you also have agreed.

Please complete the form below and return it to me as soon as possible.

Yours sincerely,
Class Teacher

....

For the parent

I am willing/not willing† for a sample of blood to be taken from my child for use in a science lesson.

Signed ....
(Parent or Guardian)
Date ....

† Please cross out the one that does not apply

....

For the child (This section need not be completed until the lesson)

I agree that the teacher may prick my finger to obtain a drop of blood.

Signed ....
Date ....

Appendix B

This Appendix lists all the major hazards which have been reported in *The School Science Review* from its first publication in 1919 to 1979 and in *Education in Science* since its first publication as the *Bulletin* of the Association for Science Education. Hazards reported in *Education in Science* are cited in italics.

It is envisaged that it will provide a handy source of reference for teachers and students, both for identifying those hazards which have been reported and as a record of various improved experimental procedures useful in school science teaching.

Although most of the principal hazards have been reported from time to time, the sources quoted in the Bibliography will be found helpful in any more exhaustive search.

The hazards reported in this Appendix are classified using the nomenclature adopted in the original source. In cases where doubt or confusion may arise, systematic names are also given and appropriate cross-references provided.

Compound, Substance, Subject	Details, Reaction etc.	Author	Reference
Accidents	Advice on insurance position	–	*1967, 23, 30*
Accidents	Some legal advice	E. A. Philpots	1933, 56, **14**, 488
Accidents	Safeguards: comprehensive article	C. W. W. Read	1940, 83, **21**, 964
Accidents and incidents	Article—General survey of accidents	–	1928, 38, **10**, 97
Acetal (1,1-diethoxy-ethane)	Explosive under distillation	A. J. Mee	1940, 85, **22**, 95
Acetates (ethanoates)	Cacodyl experiment	C. W. W. Read	1940, 83, **21**, 969
Acetic acid (ethanoic acid)	Preparation by oxidation of ethyl alcohol: explosion on distilling product	E. N. Annable	1951, 117, **32**, 249
Acetic acid, glacial	Phosphorus trichloride. Preparation of acetyl chloride. Report of explosion	T. A. H. Peacocke	1962, 152, **44**, 217
Acetic anhydride (ethanoic anhydride)	Preparation	C. W. W. Read	1940, 83, **21**, 976
Acetone	*See* Propanone		
Acetyl chloride (ethanoyl chloride)	Preparation	C. W. W. Read	1940, 83, **21**, 976

Compound, Substance, Subject	Details, Reaction etc.	Author	Reference
Acetyl peroxide	Explosive when crystallizing small quantity	A. J. Mee	1940, 85, **22**, 95
Acetylene (ethyne)	Respect under pressure, storage	F. Johnstone	1941, 88, **22**, 448
Acetylene (ethyne)	Chlorine: 'a safe way of performing'	F. Johnstone	1931, 47, **12**, 296
Acetylene (ethyne)	Chlorine	C. W. W. Read	1940, 83, **21**, 977
Acetylene (ethyne)	Copper. Explosive compounds. Copper must not be used in oxy-acetylene blowlamp	R. H. Smith	1936, 70, **18**, 281
Acetylene (ethyne)	Oxygen. Explosion	G. Fowles	1940, 85, **22**, 6
Acetylene (ethyne)	Oxygen. Explosion: extreme danger	C. Holt	1962, 152, **44**, 161
Acetylene (ethyne)	Oxygen. Violent explosion on ignition	P. D. Arculus	1963, 154, **44**, 706
Acetylene (ethyne)	Oxygen. Explosion: precautions	T. A. H. Peacocke	1964, 156 **45**, 459
Acids	Mineral. Toxic	C. G. Vernon	1927, 34, **9**, 97
Acids	Reports of accidents	—	1928, 38, **10**, 98, 102
Acids	Effect on skin	A. St. G. Huggett	1929, 41, **11**, 19
Acrolein (propenal)	Lachrymator	P. A. Ongley	1963, 154, **44**, 249
Acrylic esters (propenoates)	Some toxic	A. J. Mee	1940, 85, **42**, 95
Alcohol (ethanol)	Inflammable	C. W. W. Read	1940, 83, **21**, 973
Alcohol (ethanol)	Air oxidation to formaldehyde. Danger of ignition. Safer equipment	C. Holt	1955, 131, **37**, 135
Alcohol (ethanol)	Iodine, phosphorus, ethyl iodide preparation dangerous	C. W. W. Read	1940, 83, **21**, 967
Alkalis	Strong. Toxic	C. G. Vernon	1927, 34, **9**, 97
Alkalis	Pipetting	C. W. W. Read	1940, 83, **21**, 977
Alkaloids	Poisons	C. W. W. Read	1940, 83, **21**, 971
Alkyl fluorides	High toxicity	J. Ormston	1945, 99, **26**, 148
Allergy	Locusts, advice and warning	P. H. F. White	*1968, 28, 22*
Allyl alcohol (prop-2-en-1-ol)	Lachrymator	P. A. Ongley	1963, 154, **44**, 749
Aluminium	Ammonium nitrate. Mixture explosive	D. J. Lyness, K. Hutton	1953, 125, **35**, 139
Aluminium	Caustic alkali. Beware of hydrogen formed	D. R. Browning	1968, 168, **49**, 606
Aluminium	Sulphur	C. W. W. Read	1940, 83, **21**, 977
Aluminium	Iodine. Slight moisture results in ignition	S. Asmathullah *et al.*	1956, 134, **38**, 107
Aluminium chloride	Preparation	C. W. W. Read	1940, 83, **21**, 969
Aluminium chloride	Dust corrosive, burns caused	D. R. Browning	1967, 166, **48**, 718
Aluminium chloride	Explosion danger in sealed tubes	A. F. Kitching	1930, 45, **12**, 79
Aluminium formate (methanoate)	Explosive	A. J. Mee	1940, 85, **22**, 95
Amido derivatives of benzene	Toxic. Some are absorbed by skin	C. G. Vernon	1927, 34, **9**, 97

Compound, Substance, Subject	Details, Reaction etc.	Author	Reference
Amines, aromatic	Many suspected to be carcinogenic	D. R. Browning	1967, 167, **49**, 278
Amino alcohols	Poisons	C. W. W. Read	1940, 83, **21**, 971
Aminosulphonic acid	*See* Sulphamic acid		
Ammonia	Poison	C. W. W. Read	1940, 83, **21**, 972
Ammonia	Dangerous in case of leakage when used as refrigerant	V. A. Carpenter	1952, 120, **33**, 173
Ammonia	Beware of pressure build-up in bottles	V. A. Carpenter	1963, 154, **44**, 739
Ammonia	Preparation	C. W. W. Read	1940, 83, **21**, 976
Ammonia	Chlorine passed into. Nitrogen trichloride formed	C. W. W. Read	1940, 83, **21**, 969
Ammonia	Chlorine	C. W. W. Read	1940, 83, **21**, 976
Ammonia	Oxygen. Oxidation reaction: pass NH_3 over platinized asbestos. Beware vigorous reaction	D. Nealy	1935, 63, **16**, 410
Ammonia	Oxygen. Oxygen bubbled through NH_3	E. J. Williams	1935, 63, **16**, 410
Ammonia	Oxygen. Platinum spiral catalyst. Safe but violent	L. T. Taylor	1935, 63, **16**, 410
Ammonia	Burns in oxygen	C. W. W. Read	1940, 83, **21**, 976
Ammonia	Burns in oxygen. Details of experiment	H. D. Marshall	1968, 168, **49**, 504
Ammonia	Silver oxide ppt. When hot, explosion. Fulminate possibly formed. *See* Ammonium, Silver	J. R. Morse	1955, 131, **37**, 147
Ammonia	Catalytic oxidation. Hazardous advice in textbook	—	*1979, 84, 34*
Ammonia	Explosion when preparing and reducing copper oxide	M. A. McElroy	*1971, 71, 21*
Ammonium compounds	Sodium hydroxide boiling with	C. W. W. Read	1940, 83, **21**, 969
Ammonium dichromate(VI)	Explosive when mixed with Mg.	—	*1972, 47, 24* and *1974, 56, 39*
Ammonium dichromate(VI)	Decomposition hazardous	—	*1979, 83, 20*
Ammonium ions	Silver. Heated with NaOH to expel ammonia; Devarda's alloy added: violent explosion	J. Baldwin	1967, 165, **48**, 586
Ammonium nitrate	Heat. Explosive above 240 °C	—	1927, 34, **9**, 127
Ammonium nitrate	Extensive details of reaction	E. Coddington	1928, 35, **9**, 209
Ammonium nitrate	Explosion possible	E. A. Philpots	1933, 56, **14**, 489
Ammonium nitrate	Unpredictable explosive behaviour	S. I. Levy	1936, 68, **17**, 496
Ammonium nitrate	Heat	C. W. W. Read	1940, 83, **21**, 968
Ammonium nitrate	Heat	C. W. W. Read	1940, 83, **21**, 976
Ammonium nitrate	Aluminium. Mixture explosive	D. J. Lyness, K. Hutton	1953, 125, **35**, 139
Ammonium nitrate	Thermal decomposition. Report of details including ___ osion	J. H. Lee	1965, 160, **46**, 697
Amyl nitrate (pentyl nitrate)	Toxic; blood rush to head when inhaled	C. G. Vernon	1927, 34, **9**, 97

Compound, Substance, Subject	Details, Reaction etc.	Author	Reference
Aniline (phenylamine)	Toxic, absorbed by skin	C. G. Vernon	1927, 34, **9**, 97
		E. Hough	1968, 168, **49**, 607
Aniline (phenylamine)	Inhalation of vapour and absorption through skin—consequences	D. R. Browning	1967, 166, **48**, 718
Antimonial compounds	Poisons	C. W. W. Read	1940, 83, **21**, 971
Arsenic compounds	Toxic	C. G. Vernon	1927, 34, **9**, 97
Arsenic compounds	Poison	E. A. Philpots	1933, 56, **14**, 489
Arsenic compounds	Biological methylation of	F. Challenger	1936, 68, **17**, 575 et seq.
Arsenic compounds	Poisons	C. W. W. Read	1940, 83, **21**, 971
Arsine, chlor-diphenylamine diphenyl chlor- diphenyl cyano-	Nose irritants	F. F. Crossley	1940, 84, **21**, 1049
Asbestos	Suspected carcinogenic	D. R. Browning	1967, 167, **49**, 278
Asbestos	Calcium, molten, dropped on asbestos square caused explosion	P. J. Scott	1967, 167, **49**, 251
Asbestos	Explosion when heating solder on asbestos mat	R. D. Harris	1967, 166, **48**, 853
Asbestos	McKechnie fibre substitute	A. Cochrane	1979, 81, 26
Asbestos	Types and hazards	—	1975, 64, 16
Asbestos paper	Combustion spoon substitute	—	1977, 75, 26
Asbestos substitute	See Rocksil		
Asbestos wool	Hazards of	—	1968, 26, 28
Azides	Explosive	W. E. Garner	1933, 55, **14**, 247
Bacteriological cultures	Advice on spp.	K. M. Jack et al.	1969, 31, 29–30
Barium azide	Explosive	W. E. Garner	1933, 55, **14**, 250
Barium salts	Except sulphate, poisonous	C. W. W. Read	1940, 83, **21**, 971
Barium salts	Poisonous	A. Adair	1964, 156, **45**, 460
Battery	Explosion on recharging an expendable battery	J. Lewis	1976, 69, 21
Benzene	Inflammable	C. W. W. Read	1940, 83, **21**, 973
Benzene	Fire risk when distilling	A. W. Wellings	1941, 88, **42**, 430
Benzene	May lead to leukaemia	D. R. Browning	1967, 166, **48**, 918
Benzene	Suspected carcinogenic	D. R. Browning	1967, 167, **49**, 278
Benzene	Blood disease caused	D. R. Browning	1967, 166, **48**, 718
Benzene	Toxic, absorbed by skin	A. W. Bamford	1970, 177, **51**, 957
Benzene	Nitric acid, fuming; Nitrobenzene prepn.	—	1928, 38, **10**, 98
Benzene	Phosgene; benzophenone preparation relatively safe on small scale	J. T. Stock M. A. Fill	1961, 149, **43**, 130
Benzene	D.E.S. advice	—	1974, 58, 22
Benzene-1,3-diol	See Resorcinol		
Benzene-1,2-dicarboxylic anhydride	See Phthalic anhydride		
Benzene and some homologues	Toxic	C. G. Vernon	1927, 34, **9**, 97

Compound, Substance, Subject	Details, Reaction etc.	Author	Reference
Benzidine (biphenyl-4,4'-diamine)	Suspected carcinogenic	D. R. Browning	1967, 167, **49**, 278
Benzoyl peroxide	Advice	—	*1967, 25, 26*
Benzyl chloride	*See* (chloromethyl)benzene		
Benzyl chloride (chloromethyl)benzene	Preparation to be avoided?	C. W. W. Read	1940, 83, **21**, 969
Beryllium	Highly poisonous, acute lung disease	P. A. Philbrick	1950, 114, **31**, 263
Beryllium	Poisoning details	H. F. Boulind	1950, 115, **31**, 415
Beryllium	Poisoning. Precautions similar to those for radioactive material reqd.	N. F. Hall	1964, 158, **46**, 32
Beryllium and compounds	Health hazard described. Dust or vapour often proves fatal	H. L. Walker	1954, 127, **35**, 351
Beryllium fluoride	Magnesium. Violently exothermic	H. L. Walker	1954, 127, **35**, 348
Bleaching powder	Liable to explode if stored in warm	G. Fowles	1937, 73, **19**, 23
Blood sampling	Recommended procedures	—	*1979, 82, 27–28*
Bracken	Poisonous	H. G. Andrew	*1976, 201, 57, 783*
Brick solvent store	Danger from excessive heat or cold	R. J. Mitchell	*1979, 82, 29*
Bromide, ethyl (bromoethane)	Preparation of, using phosphorus	C. W. W. Read	1940, 83, **21**, 976
Bromine	A suggested first-aid treatment	—	1929, 41, **11**, 20
Bromine	Poison	E. A. Philpots	1933, 56, **14**, 489
Bromine	Absorption by respirator	C. L. Bryant	1940, 83, **21**, 913
Bromine	Corrosive	C. W. W. Read	1940, 83, **21**, 973
Bromine	Sixth formers and teachers only to use it	C. W. W. Read	1940, 83, **21**, 976
Bromine	Persistent and non-persistent gas	E. A. Wilson	1943, 94, **24**, 335
Bromine	Liquid causes severe and slow-healing burns	G. W. Young	1952, 120, **33**, 244
Bromine	Corrosive	P. A. Ongley	1963, 154, **44**, 747
Bromine	Keep clear of skin	T. C. Swinfen	1965, 160, **46**, 669
Bromine	Disposal of in fume cupboard	W. S. Motz	1966, 164, **48**, 179
Bromine	Preparation of	C. W. W. Read	1940, 83, **21**, 976
Bromine	Molten lead bromide electrolysis, bromine liberated. Hazardous; precautions described	C. A. Pryke	1967, 166, **48**, 862
Bromine	Ethyl bromide preparation dangerous	C. W. W. Read	1940, 83, **21**, 967
Bromine	Gallium: violent combination at room temperature	H. L. Walker	1956, 132, **37**, 196
Bromine	Organic preparations. Possible danger in handling. Small-scale experiment described	J. H. Wilkinson N. Ferry	1953, 125, **35**, 122
Bromine	Phosphorus, water. Explosion danger	A. J. Mee	1940, 85, **22**, 95
Bromine trifluoride	Well ventilated fume cupboard needed to handle	J. M. Fletcher	1952, 120, **33**, 158

Compound, Substance, Subject	Details, Reaction etc.	Author	Reference
Bromoacetates (bromo-ethanoates)	Lachrymators	P. A. Ongley	1963, 154, **44**, 747
Bromobenzene	Preparation to be avoided?	C. W. W. Read	1940, 83, **21**, 969
Bromoethane	*See* Ethyl bromide		
Burning gases at jets	More appropriate for teachers to perform than pupils	C. W. W. Read	1940, 83, **21**, 977
Butane	Gas cartridge. Beware of high temperature near cartridge	J. I. Fell	1963, 154, **44**, 728
Calcium	Asbestos. Molten calcium dropped on asbestos square caused explosion	P. J. Scott	1967, 167, **49**, 251
Calcium hypochlorite	Can cause burns	D. R. Browning	1968, 168, **49**, 606
Calcium phosphide	Explosion of bottle	—	*1970, 36, 41–42*
Carbon dioxide	Poisonous in large doses	W. L. Clark	1945, 99, **26**, 219
Carbon disulphide	Burning. Precautions	J. A. Cochrane	1928, 35, **9**, 234
Carbon disulphide	Explosion possible	E. A. Philpots	1933, 56, **14**, 489
Carbon disulphide	Inflammable	C. W. W. Read	1940, 83, **21**, 973
Carbon disulphide	Poisonous, explosive	A. J. Mee	1940, 85, **22**, 95
Carbon disulphide	Danger of explosive mixture of vapour with air	A. Towers	1948, 109, **29**, 307
Carbon disulphide	Highly explosive	G. A. Dickens	1950, 114, **31**, 264
Carbon disulphide	Further details, concerning ignition temperature	A. Webster	1950, 115, **31**, 415
Carbon disulphide	Inflammable, narcotic	D. R. Browning	1967, 166, **48**, 718
Carbon disulphide	Burn nitric oxide with	C. W. W. Read	1940, 83, **21**, 977
Carbon disulphide	Nitric oxide, burns with blue flash	F. A. Halton	1963, 154, **44**, 701
Carbon disulphide	Survey of hazards	D. M. Wharry	1973, 191, **55**, 417
Carbon monosulphide	Readily polymerizes with explosive violence	T. G. Pearson	1938, 78, **20**, 189
Carbon monoxide	Toxic	C. G. Vernon	1927, 34, **9**, 97
Carbon monoxide	Poison	E. A. Philpots	1933, 56, **14**, 489
Carbon monoxide	Poison	F. Briers	1935, 65, **17**, 36
Carbon monoxide	Prepare in small quantities only	C. W. W. Read	1940, 83, **21**, 969
Carbon monoxide	Poison	C. W. W. Read	1940, 83, **21**, 973
Carbon monoxide	Preparation	C. W. W. Read	1940, 83, **21**, 976
Carbon monoxide	Volume composition of	C. W. W. Read	1940, 83, **21**, 976
Carbon monoxide	Explosion when made from C + O_2	W. E. Jones	*1967, 23, 42–43* and *1967, 21, 47–48*
Carbon monoxide	Explosion when made from HCOOH	—	*1972, 46, 22*
Carbon suboxide	Preparation. Gas poisonous	D. B. Briggs	1931, 48, **12**, 380
Carbon tetrachloride (tetrachloromethane)	Extinguishers. Oxidation to phosgene in confined spaces	R. W. Thomas	1965, 160, **46**, 775
Carbon tetrachloride	Damage may prove fatal. Details	D. R. Browning	1967, 166, **48**, 718
Carbon tetrachloride	Fumes	D. R. Browning	1967, 166, **48**, 918
Carbon tetrachloride	Alternative in preparing SnI_4	M. A. Coles *et al.*	*1977, 206, 59, 158* and *1978, 208, 59, 561*

Compound, Substance, Subject	Details, Reaction etc.	Author	Reference
Carbonyl chloride	*See* Phosgene		
Carbylamine test	Teachers' opinions on its use	C. W. W. Read	1940, 83, **21**, 969, 976
Carcinogenesis	Substances causing	D. R. Browning	1968, 168, **49**, 607
Carcinogens	Survey of hazards	—	*1979, 84, 17–21*
Carius expts.	Should not be conducted in schools	C. W. W. Read	1940, 83, **21**, 977
Charcoal	Sulphur, potassium nitrate. Grind: explosive	—	1923, 18, **5**, 112
Charcoal blocks	Fire risk	C. W. W. Read	1940, 83, **21**,969
Chlorate mixture	Discussion on use of as fuse in Thermit process	Editors of *Science Master's Book*, IV, 2	1966, 162, **47**, 560
Chlorate mixtures	Dangerously sensitive	H. K. Black	1963, 153, **44**,462
Chlorates	Explosion possible. *See also* Potassium chloride	E. A. Philpots	1933, 56, **14**, 489
Chlorhydrin	Potentially toxic	A. J. Mee	1940, 85, **22**, 96
Chloric(VII) acid	*See* Perchloric acid		
Chlorides, anhydrous	Preparation	C. W. W. Read	1940, 83, **21**, 976
Chlorine	Toxic	C. G. Vernon	1927, 34, **9**, 97
Chlorine	Poison	—	1929, 41, **11**, 22
Chlorine	Poison	E. A. Philpots	1933, 56, **14**, 489
Chlorine	Poison	C. W. W. Read	1940, 83, **21**, 973
Chlorine	Lung irritant	F. F. Crossley	1940, 84, **21**, 1049
Chlorine	Gassing danger	C. W. W. Read	1941, 87, **22**, 340
Chlorine	Preparation	C. W. W. Read	1940, 83, **21**, 976
Chlorine	Preparation by dropping conc. hydrochloric acid on $KMnO_4$: explosion reported	J. C. Curry	1965, 160, **46**, 770
Chlorine	Preparation and preservation of LIQUID chlorine at room temperature	J. G. Silcock	1968, 168, **49**, 496
Chlorine	Acetylene. 'A safe way of performing?'	—	1931, 47, **12**, 296
Chlorine	Acetylene	C. W. W. Read	1940, 83, **21**, 977
Chlorine	Ammonia. Passed into NH_3 soln. Nitrogen trichloride formed	C. W. W. Read	1940, 83, **21**, 969
Chlorine	Ammonia	C. W. W. Read	1940, 83, **21**, 976
Chlorine	Hydrogen, explosion with	C. W. W. Read	1940, 83, **21**, 969, 976
Chlorine	Hydrogen, explosion with. Precautions needed, e.g. avoid sunlight	J. Lambert	1948, 109, **29**, 364
Chlorine	Hydrogen. Explosion on thorough mixing on dull day	L. H. Angus	1950, 115, **31**, 402
Chlorine	Hydrogen, explosion with	C. Holt	1962, 152, **44**, 161
Chlorine	Hydrogen, explosion with: precautions	T. A. H. Peacocke	1964, 156, **45**, 459
Chlorine	Hydrogen. Photocatalytic explosion demonstration	A. Adair	1966, 164, **48**, 159
Chlorine	Methane. Sometimes explosive violence	G. H. James	1966, 164, **48**, 46

Compound, Substance, Subject	Details, Reaction etc.	Author	Reference
Chlorine	Methyl alcohol. Fire	A. J. Mee	1940, 85, **42**, 96
Chlorine	Soda, molten. Dangerous	J. Bradley	1968, 168, **49**, 454
Chlorine trifluoride	Well ventilated fume cupboard needed to handle	J. M. Fletcher	1952, 120, **33**, 158
Chlorobenzene	Avoid preparation?	C. W. W. Read	1940, 83, **21**, 969
Chlorodinitrobenzene	Beware. Special note on vapour when in solution	C. G. Vernon	1927, 34, **9**, 98
1-chloro-2,4-dinitrobenzene	Potent sensitizer	—	1977, 204, **58**, 582
Chloroform (trichloromethane)	Poison	C. W. W. Read	1940, 83, **21**, 972
Chloroform	Photochemical oxidation in air, giving phosgene	P. F. R. Venables	1942, 92, **24**, 26
Chloroform	Anaesthetic. Causes conjunctivitis, poisonous by mouth	D. R. Browning	1967, 166, **48**, 718
Chloroform	Sodium, violent reaction with	D. R. Browning	1967, 166, **48**, 718
Chloroform	Explosion on mixing with propanone	E. H. Coulson	1974, 192, **55**, 596
Chloroform	Explosion with propanone	—	*1974, 57, 38*
(Chloromethyl)benzene	Possible carcinogen	D. Hodgson	*1974, 58, 32*
Chloropicrin (trichloronitromethane)	Lung irritant	F. F. Crossley	1940, 84, **21**, 1049
Chlorosilanes	Hydrolysis strongly exothermic, severe burns caused to skin, very inflammable, plant unit kept under small positive pressure of nitrogen	S. J. Hart	1959, 141, **40**, 260
Chloro-vinyl-dichlorarsine (Lewisite)	Vesicant	F. F. Crossley	1940, 84, **21**, 1049
Chromates, dichromates	Absorption: disease, results, details	D. R. Browning	1967, 166, **48**, 718
Coal dust	Explosion	F. Briers	1935, 65, **17**, 36
Coal dust	Details for performing experimental 'safe' explosions	W. Railston	1937, 74, **19**, 173
Coal gas	Toxicity should not be exaggerated	G. Fowles	1940, 85, **22**, 5
Coal gas	'Deadly poison'	C. W. W. Read	1941, 87, **22**, 341
Coal gas	Possible explosion	E. A. Philpots	1933, 56, **14**, 489
Coal gas	Poison	C. W. W. Read	1940, 83, **21**, 972
Coal gas	Bernouilli effect; precautions when showing	C. McGarry	1966, 162, **42**, 504
Coal gas	Reduction of oxides	C. W. W. Read	1940, 83, **21**, 976
Coal gas, oxygen blow pipe	Warnings about, e.g. explosion, fire, melted metals	G. W. Young	1948, 109, **29**, 368
Coal tar	Fractional distillation yields poisonous corrosive phenolic products	M. S. Parker	1965, 159, **46**, 345
Commercial chemicals	How 'safe' are they?	C. W. W. Read	1940, 83, **21**, 977
Conservation of matter	Enclosed experiments for	C. W. W. Read	1940, 83, **21**, 977
Copper	Acetylene. Explosive compound, therefore copper must not be used for oxyacetylene blow lamps	R. H. Smith	1936, 70, **18**, 281

Compound, Substance, Subject	Details, Reaction etc.	Author	Reference
Copper	Hydrochloric acid boiling. Explosion when cooled (corked flask). Possible explanation	—	1924, 21, **6,** 55
Copper	Sulphuric acid conc. Caution when adding copper to hot sulphuric acid: violent reaction	G. Fowles	1927, 34, **9,** 90
Copper	Sulphuric acid. Dangerous preparation of SO_2	D. A. Campbell	1939, 80, **20,** 631
Copper	Sulphuric acid: SO_2 preparation	C. W. W. Read	1940, 83, **21,** 969
Copper oxalate	Explosion possible on heating	W. E. Garner	1933, 55, **14,** 247
Copper oxide	Anhydrous, with phthalic anhydride: explosive when overheated	A. J. Mee	1940, 85, **22,** 95
Copper oxide	Reduction by hydrogen. Explosion	C. W. W. Read	1941, 87, **22,** 340
Copper oxide	In Thermit process: explosion	T. E. W. Browne	1967, 166, **48,** 921
Copper(II) oxide	Reduction by CO; explosion	—	*1972, 46, 22*
Copper(II) oxide	Reduction by NH_3 explosion	M. A. McElroy	*1979, 71, 21*
Creosote	Poison	C. W. W. Read	1940, 83, **21,** 972
Critical state expt.	Danger of tube 'blow out': minimization of danger	W. K. Mace	1957, 136, **38,** 466
Critical state expt.	Precautions for handling tubes at high pressure	I. W. Jones *et al.*	1962, 152, **44,** 173
Crude oil	*See* petroleum		
Cyanide, hydrogen	Not recommended	A. W. Wellings	1941, 88, **22,** 429
Cyanide, potassium	Use only by teachers	C. W. W. Read	1940, 83, **21,** 976
Cyanides	Poison	E. A. Philpots	1933, 56, **14,** 489
Cyanides	Poison: precautions	—	1935, 65, **17,** 146
Cyanides	Poison	C. W. W. Read	1940, 83, **21,** 972
Cyanides	Toxic	P. A. Ongley	1963, 154, **44,** 747
Cyanides	Danger of using such highly poisonous solution as electrolyte	F. E. L. Parsons	1935, 66, **17,** 179
Cyanogen	Preparation	C. W. W. Read	1940, 83, **21,** 977
Cyanogen compounds	Toxic	C. G. Vernon	1927, 34, **9,** 97
Cyclotron	Neutrons emitted: possible harmful effects	R. Pardoe	1944, 97, **25,** 286
Cylinders	*See* Gas cylinders		
Detergent	*See* sodium		
Detonations and solid reactions	Review of a paper	—	1935, 65, **17,** 150
Devarda's alloy	Silver and ammonium ions. NaOH, heat to expel NH_3. Addition of alloy caused violent explosion	J. Baldwin	1967, 165, **48,** 586
Dichloro-diethyl sulphide (mustard gas)	Vesicant	F. F. Crossley	1940, 84, **21,** 1049
Dichromates	Absorption-disease, details	D. R. Browning	1967, 166, **48,** 718
1,1-Diethoxyethane	*See* Acetal		
Di-isocyanates	Extreme toxicity	E. G. Meek	1975, 198, **57,** 187
Dimethyl sulphate	Lung and sight injury	D. R. Browning	1967, 166, **48,** 718

Compound, Substance, Subject	Details, Reaction etc.	Author	Reference
Dinitro compounds	Poison	C. W. W. Read	1940, 83, **21**, 971
Dinitrobenzene	Beware of on skin	C. G. Vernon	1927, 34, **9**, 97
2,4-dinitrobenzene	Powerful sensitizer	—	1976, 67, 15
2,4-dinitrofluorobenzene	Powerful sensitizer	—	1976, 67, 15
Dinitrophenol	Beware of on skin	C. G. Vernon	1927, 34, **9**, 97
Dioxan (diethyl dioxide)	Particularly explosive	G. N. Copley	1939, 82, **21**, 871
Dioxan (diethyl dioxide)	Potentially toxic	A. J. Mee	1940, 85, **22**, 95
Diphenyl chlor-arsine	Nose irritant	F. F. Crossley	1940, 84, **21**,1049
Diphenyl cyanoarsine	Nose irritant	F. F. Crossley	1940, 84, **21**, 1049
Diphenylamine chlor-arsine	Nose irritant	F. F. Crossley	1940, 84, **21**, 1049
Dissection	Advice for schools	—	1976, 70, 25 and 1975, 64, 29
Dust explosions	Use of plastic bag	R. G. Bray	1967, 165, **48**, 510
Electrical hazards	Advice and recommendations	—	1979, 83, 20–21
Electrical sockets	Advice on testing safety of	M. D. Ellse	1977, 205, 58, 820–22
Enclosed expts. for conservation of matter	Should only be done by teachers	C. W. W. Read	1940, 83, **21**, 977
Epoxyethane	See Ethylene oxide		
Ethanedioic acid	See Oxalic acid		
Ethanol	See Ethyl alcohol		
Ethene	See Ethylene		
Ethenone	See Ketene		
Ether (ethoxyethane)	Safe for sixth formers to prepare	C. W. W. Read	1940, 83, **21**, 977
Ether (ethoxyethane)	Care	G. Fowles	1940, 85, **22**, 6
Ether (ethoxyethane)	Explosion possible	E. A. Philpots	1933, 56, **14**, 489
Ether (ethoxyethane)	Old stocks may contain much explosive peroxide	—	1937, 71, **18**, 447
Ether (ethoxyethane)	Dangers of peroxide impurity	B.D.H.	1937, 74, **19**, 189
Ether (ethoxyethane)	Evaporation by fan: ensure motor of fan does not come into contact with vapour	A. Adair	1963, 153, **44**, 418
Ether (ethoxyethane)	Recovery: peroxide risk	C. W. W. Read	1940, 83, **21**, 977
Ether, diisopropyl	Peroxide formation	G. N. Copley	1939, 82, **21**, 871
Ether peroxide	Peroxide, acetaldehyde etc. impurities in ether. Nausea caused. Explosion in case of peroxide	P. F. R. Venables	1942, 92, **24**, 26
Ether, preparation	Lower ethers hazardous because of inflammability and volatility	W. H. Dovell	1964, 156, **45**, 407
Ethers	Explosive peroxide formation, removal of	G. N. Copley	1939, 82, **21**, 871
Ethers	Explosions possible	A. J. Mee	1940, 85, **22**, 95
Ethyl alcohol (ethanol)	Oxidation to acetic acid: explosion on distilling product (see also Alcohols)	E. N. Annable	1951, 117, **32**, 249
Ethyl bromide (bromoethane)	Preparation using phosphorus	C. W. W. Read	1940, 83, **21**, 976

Compound, Substance, Subject	Details, Reaction etc.	Author	Reference
Ethyl iodide (iodoethane)	Preparation	C. W. W. Read	1940, 83, **21**, 967
Ethyl iodo-acetate (iodo-ethanoate)	Lachrymator	F. F. Crossley	1940, 84, **21**, 1049
Ethylene (ethene)	Oxygen, explosion. Precautions	T. A. H. Peacocke	1964, 156, **45**, 459
Ethylene derivatives	Volatile derivatives toxic	A. J. Mee	1940, 85, **22**, 95
Ethylene oxide (epoxy-ethane)	Toxic, potentially	A. J. Mee	1940, 85, **22**, 95
Ethyne	*See* Acetylene		
Explosions	Some potentially explosive reactions	E. A. Philpots	1933, 56, **14**, 489
Explosives	Home Office advice	—	*1965, 12, 33–34*
Explosives, nitro	—	S. I. Levy	1935, 67, **17**, 341
Explosives, nitro	—	S. I. Levy	1936, 68, **17**, 488
Eye protection	Clarification of D.E.S. advice	N. Booth	*1976, 70, 20*
Faulty apparatus	Responsibility for	—	*1976, 67, 14–15*
Ferric oxide (iron(III) oxide)	Reduction by carbon monoxide. Danger of forming explosive iron pentacarbonyl at low temps. (0–150 °C)	C. W. Othen	1964, 156, **45**, 459
Fire	Background to fire control	W. J. Leggett	1974, 195, **56**, 406
Fire extinguishers	Carbon tetrachloride type dangerous with incendiary bombs etc.: explosion phosgene	A. J. Mee	1940, 85, **22**, 95
First aid	Common first-aid procedures (some now obsolete)	—	1929, 41, **11**, 17
Fittig's reaction	Suitable for teachers or sixth formers	C. W. W. Read	1940, 83, **21**, 977
Flammable liquids	Storage advice	—	*1976, 67, 14*
Fluoride, hydrogen	High toxicity	J. Ormston	1945, 99, **26**, 148
Fluorides, alkyl	High toxicity	J. Ormston	1945, 99, **26**, 148
Fluorine	Corrosive: precautions in handling	J. M. Fletcher	1952, 120, **33**, 155
Fluorine	'The Manufacture and use of Fluorine and its Compounds'. Book review. Gives details of risk involved in school preparation of fluorine	A. J. Rudge	1962, 152, **44**, 242
Fluorine	Health hazard	H. L. Walker	1954, 127, **35**, 346
Fluorine	With hydrogen: explosive	J. M. Fletcher	1952, 120, **33**, 156
Fluorine	Organic molecules, Copper gauze catalyst used to prevent explosions, also fluorine diluted	J. Ormston	1944, 98, **26**, 30
Fluorine	Organic compounds. Explosive: vapours diluted with N_2 and reactor filled with silver-plated copper turnings	J. M. Fletcher	1952, 120, **33**, 157
Fluoroacetates (fluoroethanoates) and derivatives	Toxic, details	B. C. Saunders	1952, 121, **33**, 325

Compound, Substance, Subject	Details, Reaction etc.	Author	Reference
Fluorophosphine oxides, diamino	Toxic generally	B. C. Saunders	1952, 121, **33**, 324
Fluorophosphonates	Toxic; details	B. C. Saunders	1952, 121, **33**, 320
Food calorimeter	Explosion using peanut	I. Nuttall	1977, 205, **58**, 817
Formaldehyde (methanal)	Poison	C. W. W. Read	1940, 83, **21**, 972
Formaldehyde	Preparation from air and methyl alcohol using Cu or Pt catalyst. Explosion possible	P. H. Arnold	1952, 120, **33**, 267
Formaldehyde	Preparation: safe method	G. F. Hood	1952, 121, **33**, 416
Formaldehyde	Preparation: further details	D. T. Radford	1953, 124, **34**, 426
Formaldehyde	Resorcinol resin: explosion	—	*1971, 45, 36*
Friedel-Crafts reaction	—	C. W. W. Read	1940, 83, **21**, 977
Gallium	Bromine, violent combination at room temperature	H. L. Walker	1956, 132, **37**, 196
Gas	Hazard in preparing from oil	—	*1972, 46, 22*
Gas cylinders	Storage advice	—	*1970, 36, 47*
Gaseous explosions	'Flame and combustion in Gases'. Ref. book, deals with gaseous explosions	W. A. Bone *et al.*	1928, 37, **10**, 80
Gaseous explosions	Use of plastic bag in	R. G. Bray	1967, 165, **48**, 570
Gaseous mixtures	Explosion of: dangerous	C. W. W. Read	1940, 83, **21**, 965
Gaseous mixtures	Explosions. Method	P. D. Arculus	1963, 154, **44**, 706
Gaseous mixtures	Explosion of: use balloon	B. Poole	1964, 158, **46**, 230
Gaseous mixtures	Explosion of: details and precautions	T. A. H. Peacocke	1964, 156, **45**, 459
Gases	Explosion and fires in coal mines	F. Briers	1935, 65, **17**, 36
Gases	Explosive mixtures of	C. W. W. Read	1941, 87, **22**, 340
Gases	Flame and Combustion in. Ref. book, deals with gaseous explosions	W. A. Bone *et al.*	1928, 37, **10**, 80
Gases	Jets, burning at	C. W. W. Read	1940, 83, **21**, 977
Gases	Poisonous: coal gas, CO, CO_2, Cl_2, SO_2, H_2	—	1929, 41, **11**, 22
Gases	Poisonous: SO_2, H_2S, Cl_2, N_2O_4 NO, NH_3, Br_2, S	C. W. W. Read	1940, 83, **21**, 968
Gases	Respirator, absorption by	C. L. Bryant	1940, 83, **21**, 913
Gases	Toxic: H_2S, PH_3, CO, Cl_2, oxides of N	C. G. Vernon	1927, 34, **9**, 97
Gases	Warfare, used in	F. F. Crossley	1940, 84, **21**, 1049
Gases	Warfare, used in	E. A. Wilson	1943, 94, **24**, 335
Glass tubing	Dangers of	C. W. W. Read	1941, 87, **22**, 341
Glycerol (propane-1,2,3-triol)	Nitration of, with conc. sulphuric and nitric acids. Reaction can become uncontrollable	S. I. Levy	1935, 67, **17**, 344
Goggles	*See* Eye protection		
Groundsel	Hazards of	H. G. Andrew	*1976, 201, 57, 783*
Groundsel	*See Senecio* spp.		

Compound, Substance, Subject	Details, Reaction etc.	Author	Reference
Gunpowder	Preparation	C. W. W. Read	1940, 83, **21**, 977
Halogen acids	Can be safely prepared	G. Fowles	1940, 85, **22**, 6
Halogen acids	Preparation	C. W. W. Read	1940, 83, **21**, 977
Halogenated D.N.B.	Powerful sensitizers	—	*1976, 67, 15*
'Hazards'	B.D.H.Dealing with spillage of hazardous chemicals. Wall chart on hazards available	B.D.H.	1965, 159, **46**, 471
Health and Safety legislation	—	—	*1977, 72, 19–20*
Health and Safety legislation	A.S.E. statements	—	*1976, 66, 25* and *1975, 64, 13*
Hepatitis	Risk of, blood group determination	—	*1976, 67, 16*
Hydrazine hydrate	Poisonous	G. Fowles	1963, 154, **44**, 692
Hydrazine hydrate	Further details. Caustic	A. Adair	1964, 156, **45**, 460
Hydrocarbons, polycyclic aromatic	Carcinogenic	C. F. Cullis	1968, 168, **49**, **402**
Hydrochloric acid	Poison	C. W. W. Read	1940, 83, **21**, 972
Hydrochloric acid	Conc. on to potassium permanganate. Explosion took place	J. C. Curry	1965, 160, **46**, 770
Hydrofluoric acid	Danger to skin	—	1929, 42, **11**, 152
Hydrogen	Preparation. Sodium on water, collection	C. W. W. Read	1940, 83, **21**, 976
Hydrogen	Preparation. Acid on metal	C. W. W. Read	1940, 83, **21**, 977
Hydrogen	Preparation. Safer method using tap funnel for acid	C. Mangham	1964, 158, **46**, 233
Hydrogen	Preparation. Safe generator, burner	A. V. Pitter	1964, 157, **45**, 685
Hydrogen	Air. Why quiet burning of inverted jar?	—	1922, 14, **4**, 97
Hydrogen	Air. Reply to query above	—	1922, 16, **4**, 215
Hydrogen	Burning of	C. W. W. Read	1940, 83, **21**, 976
Hydrogen	Chlorine, explosion with	C. W. W. Read	1940, 83, **21**, 969
Hydrogen	Chlorine, explosion with	C. W. W. Read	1940, 83, **21**, 976
Hydrogen	Chlorine, explosion with: details of precautions	J. Lambert	1948, 109, **29**, 364
Hydrogen	Chlorine, explosion with. Explosion on thorough mixing on dull day	L. H. Angus	1950, 115, **31**, 402
Hydrogen	Chlorine, explosion with	C. Holt	1962, 152, **44**, 161
Hydrogen	Chlorine: explosion with: precautions	T. A. H. Peacocke	1964, 156, **45**, 459
Hydrogen	Chlorine: photocatalytic explosion demonstration	A. Adair	1966, 164, **48**, 159
Hydrogen	Fluorine, explosive	J. M. Fletcher	1952, 120, **33**, 156
Hydrogen	Jet: beware explosive mixture with air	—	1928, 38, **10**, 99
Hydrogen	Jets, danger of	E. A. Philpots	1933, 56, **14**, 489
Hydrogen	Jets. Safe methods of igniting using test tube full of collected gas	K. G. Price	1964, 158, **46**, 187

Compound, Substance, Subject	Details, Reaction etc.	Author	Reference
Hydrogen	Oxygen. Explanation why no explosion with hot silver wire	C. N. Hinshelwood	1927, 31, **8**, 171
Hydrogen	Oxygen. Explosion with certain volumes, in eudiometer: dangers	R. D. Reid	1928, 38, **10**, 149
Hydrogen	Oxygen. Form soap bubbles: harmless explosions	R. R. Finney	1935, 65, **17**, 137
Hydrogen	Oxygen. Explosions hazardous	C. W. W. Read	1940, 83, **21**, 976
Hydrogen	Oxygen. Explosion with: extra care required	C. Holt	1962, 152, **44**, 161
Hydrogen	Oxygen. Explosion with: precautions	T. A. H. Peacocke	1964, 156, **45**, 459
Hydrogen	Oxygen. Explosion with: demonstration using polythene flask	J. W. Davis	1964, 157, **45**, 649
Hydrogen	Oxygen. Explosion with: demonstration using polythene bottle	E. V. Ogden	1964, 157, **45**,674
Hydrogen	Oxygen. Explosion with: use balloon	B. Poole	1964, 158, **46**, 230
Hydrogen	Oxygen. Explosion with: 'Safe experiment' described	M. J. Clark	1965, 161, **47**, 177
Hydrogen	Reduction of copper oxide by	C. W. W. Read	1941, 87, **22**, 340
Hydrogen	Reduction of metal oxides: dangerous	C. W. W. Read	1940, 83, **21**, 965
Hydrogen	Reduction of oxides	C. W. W. Read	1940, 83, **21**, 976
Hydrogen	Reduction of oxides: method of avoiding danger	H. E. Watson	1943, 93, **24**, 211
Hydrogen	Danger when used as reductant	—	*1970, 40, 32,*
Hydrogen	Relative merits of thistle and tap funnel in preparation	—	*1975, 61, 33*
Hydrogen chloride	Vapour: industrial absorption	S. I. Levy	1934, 62, **16**, 154
Hydrogen chloride	Respiratory damage caused	D. R. Browning	1967, 166, **48**, 718
Hydrogen cyanide	Sex-linked ability to smell	G. J. Cooper	*1967, 24, 33*
Hydrogen fluoride	Risk of burns can be reduced, although very dangerous to handle	A. J. Rudge	1962, 151, **43**, 672
Hydrogen fluoride	High toxicity	J. Ormston	1945, 99, **26**, 148
Hydrogen fluoride	Mercuric oxide. Mercuric fluoride produced reacts with organic molecules: highly exothermic reaction	J. Ormston	1944, 98, **26**, 32
Hydrogen sulphide	Toxic	C. G. Vernon	1927, 34, **9**, 97
Hydrogen sulphide	Poison	F. Briers	1935, 65, **17**, 36
Hydrogen sulphide	Poison	C. W. W. Read	1940, 83, **21**, 973
Hydrogen sulphide	Poisonous	A. W. Wellings	1942, 92, **24**, 83
Hydrogen sulphide	Toxic	B. E. Dawson	1961, 147, **42**, 214
Hydrogen sulphide	Toxicity comparable to hydrogen cyanide	D. R. Browning	1967, 166, **48**, 919
Hydrogen sulphide	High concentrations fatal; inflammable	D. R. Browning	1967, 166, **48**, 718
Hydrogen sulphide	Ignited by trace of Na_2O_2 or rusty pipes	A. J. Mee	1940, 85, **22**, 95

Compound, Substance, Subject	Details, Reaction etc.	Author	Reference
Hydrogen sulphide	Preparation; synthesis, use of	C. W. W. Read	1940, 83, **21**, 976
Hydrogenation	Catalytic. Hershberg apparatus. Exclusion of air vital, otherwise explosion over catalyst. Safety screen advisable	—	1966, 163, **47**, 808
Ice	Caution needed in dislodging	M. A. McElroy	*1977, 71, 21*
Immersion heater	Explosion of	K. A. Hall	*1979, 84, 34*
Incendiary bombs etc.	Carbon tetrachloride extinguisher may cause explosion and large quantities of phosgene	A. J. Mee	1940, 85, **22**, 95
Infra red lamps	Water, speck of, causes implosion	A. T. Neuff	1967, 165, **48**, 489
Iodine	Aluminium: slight moisture results in ignition	S. Azmathullah	1956, 134, **38**, 107
Iodine	Phosphorus, alcohol: ethyl iodide preparation dangerous	C. W. W. Read	1940, 83, **21**, 967
Iodoethane	*See* Ethyl iodide		
Iodomethane	Cancer hazard	D. Hodgson	*1974, 58, 32*
Ion-exchange resin	Hazards of soaking a dry resin	P. Rankin	*1976, 67, 15*
Iron	Steam on red-hot iron	C. W. W. Read	1940, 83, **21**, 976
Iron	Filings, sulphuric acid: $FeSO_4$ prepn.	C. W. W. Read	1940, 83, **21**, 969
Iron(III) oxide	*See* Ferric oxide		
Kaowool	Disadvantages as asbestos substitute	D. A. Tawney	*1978, 79, 32*
Kaowool	Disadvantages of	M. Tingle T. Goodfellow	*1978, 77, 21–22*
Ketene (ethenone)	Poisonous, but destroyed by water	J. W. Davis	1952, 121, **33**, 396
Labelling	A.S.E. advice	—	*1979, 82, 25–26*
Laboratory check list	*See* Safety check list		
Laboratory Rules	Mnemonic	I. M. Carpenter	1977, 205, **58**, 817
Lassaigne test	Source of danger. Microtechnique to minimize danger; other precautions, *see* Sodium	J. T. Stock M. A. Fill	1956, 133, **37**, 346
Lauroyl peroxide	Additive to render safer	—	*1967, 21, 26*
Lead bromide	Electrolysis of molten. Hazardous. Bromine, lead bromide vapours. Precautions	C. A. Pryke	1967, 166, **48**, 862
Lead compounds	Toxic	C. G. Vernon	1927, 34, **9**, 97
Lead compounds	Poison	C. W. W. Read	1940, 83, **21**, 972
Lead nitrate	Potassium acetate: mixture explosive when heated	A. J. Mee	1940, 85, **22**, 95
Lithium	Explosion on heating	W. H. Lloyd	1975, 196, **56**, 632
Lithium	Explosion on heating	C. Holt	1975, 198, **57**, 185
Lithium	Explosion when heated on ceramic material	—	*1975, 62, 29*
Lithium	Explosion when heated on porcelain	A. Bullock	*1975, 62, 33*
Locust allergy	*See* allergy		

Compound, Substance, Subject	Details, Reaction etc.	Author	Reference
Magnesium	Beryllium fluoride: violently exothermic	H. L. Walker	1954, 127, **35**, 348
Magnesium	Oxygen: burning magnesium in oxygen	C. W. W. Read	1940, 83, **21**, 968
Magnesium	Potassium carbonate: explosive substance produced	J. G. F. Druce	1926, 28, **7**, 261
Magnesium	Potassium carbonate: Castellana fusion, possible explosion	G. Fowles	1938, 77, **20**, 124
Magnesium	Silica: denotation if silica not completely dry	W. B. Barker	1938, 77, **20**, 150
Magnesium	Powder, silver nitrate powder. Explosion with drop of water	D. J. Lyness K. Hutton	1953, 125, **35**, 138
Magnesium	Steam: method avoiding difficulties	J. D. Peterkin	1934, 60, **15**, 524
Magnesium	Steam: explosion possible with hydrogen if any undisplaced air in apparatus	T. A. Muir	1936, 70, **18**, 283
Magnesium	Steam	C. W. W. Read	1940, 83, **21**, 976
Magnesium	Steam: simple apparatus for burning in	E. A. Taylor	1940, 84, **21**, 1143
Magnesium	Sulphur	C. W. W. Read	1940, 83, **21**, 977
Magnesium	Sulphur. Heat: explosion	K. Hutton	1950, 114, **31**, 265
Magnesium	Explosive silicide on heating in porcelain crucible	R. B. Moyes *et al.*	1975, 197, **56**, 819
Magnesium	Explosive mixture with ammonium dichromate(VI)	—	*1972, 47, 24* and *1974, 56, 39*
Mains Leads	Hazards if uncoiled	W. K. Mace	1977, 204, **58**, 587
Manganese	Production by Thermit process	G. Fowles	1940, 85, **22**, 6
Manganese dioxide (manganese(IV) oxide)	Oxygen preparation: pure samples usable	H. Tattersall	1956, 134, **38**, 132
Marsh's test	Survey of its use	C. W. W. Read	1940, 83, **21**, 976
Mercuric oxide (mercury(II) oxide)	Hydrogen fluoride. Mercuric fluoride produced reacts with organic molecules highly exothermically	J. Ormston	1944, 98, **26**, 32
Mercuric sulphate (mercury(II) sulphate)	Preparation	C. W. W. Read	1940, 83, **21**, 969
Mercury	Harmful vapour	H. L. Walker	1956, 132, **37**, 198
Mercury	Toxic, high vapour pressure	J. A. Plewes	1964, 157, **45**, 717
Mercury	Continues to vaporize when covered with water	P. J. Weeks	*1977, 73, 24*
Mercury	Degree of hazard not to be overestimated	F. G. Scrawley	*1977, 74, 25*
Mercury	Advice on recovery of	D. Hodson	*1972, 46, 22–23*
Mercury	Precautions in use of	T. P. Borrows	*1977, 72, 20–21* and 1978, 209, **59**, 750–2
Mercury and compounds	Toxic	N. F. Hall	1964, 158, **46**, 32
Mercury compounds	Toxic	C. G. Vernon	1927, 34, **9**, 97
Mercury compounds	Poison	C. W. W. Read	1940, 83, **21**, 972
Mercury oxalate	Likely to explode on heating	W. E. Garner	1933, 55, **14**, 247

Compound, Substance, Subject	Details, Reaction etc.	Author	Reference
Methanal	*See* Formaldehyde		
Methane	Fire, explosion	F. Briers	1935, 65, **17**, 36
Methane	Explosion danger	J. A. Stevenson	1946, 102, **27**, 170
Methane	Air, dangerously explosive mixtures	J. H. Wilkinson	1962, 152, **44**, 4
Methane	Chlorine: sometimes explosive violence	G. H. James	1966, 164, **48**, 46
Methane	Oxygen: explosive reactions possible	T. G. Pearson	1940, 83, **21**, 923
Methane	Oxygen, explosions with: precautions	T. A. H. Peacocke	1964, 156, **45**, 459
Methyl alcohol (methanol)	Air, mixture with: over Cu or Pt catalyst. Formaldehyde preparation. Explosion possible	P. H. Arnold	1953, 120, **33**, 267
Methyl alcohol	Air mixture with: over Cu. Safe expt. described	G. F. Hood	1952, 121, **33**, 416
Methyl alcohol	Air, mixture with: further details	D. T. Radford	1953, 124, **34**, 426
Methyl alcohol	Modifications of catalytic oxidation: 'harmless explosions'	D. T. Radford	1956, 132, **37**, 258
Methylbenzene	*See* Toluene		
Methyl bromide (bromomethane)	Toxic. Precautions in preparation	S.M.A. Meeting report	1956, 133, **37**, 408
Methyl-2,4,6-trinitrobenzene	*See* Toluene and homologues and Trinitrotoluene		
Microbiology	Details of advisory committee for schools	—	*1976, 67, 23*
Millon's reagent	Hazards and possible substitute	—	*1979, 83, 19–20*
Millon's reagent	Sakaguchi test as substitute	—	*1979, 85, 31*
Naphthylamine (naphthalen-1-amine)	Inappropriate for phase rule studies	D. R. Browning	1967, 166, **48**, 719
Naphthylamines	Carcinogenic	D. R. Browning	1967, 167, **49**, 278
Natural gas	Problems of burning	P. Stone	*1977, 71, 21–22*
Natural gas	Explosion in air	T. P. Borrows	1978, 209, **59**, 752
Neutrons	Harmful effect of; from cyclotron	R. Pardoe	1944, 97, **25**, 286
Nickel, Raney	Precautions; pyrophoric when dry	A. Adair	1963, 153, **44**, 417
Nickel carbonyl	Formation and decomposition. Extremely toxic. 1 part in 10^6 in air fatal	D. C. M. Waddell	1966, 164, **48**, 167
Nitric acid	Burns	C. G. Vernon	1928, 38, **10**, 97
Nitric acid	Poison	C. W. W. Read	1940, 83, **21**, 972
Nitric acid	Poison	D. R. Browning	1968, 168, **49**, 606
Nitric acid	Preparation	C. W. W. Read	1940, 83, **21**, 976
Nitric acid	Heat: decompose	C. W. W. Read	1940, 83, **21**, 977
Nitric acid	Oxidation of solids by	C. W. W. Read	1940, 83, **21**, 976
Nitric acid	Hazards of reaction with ether	C. Holt	1976, 202, **58**, 159–160
Nitric(V) acid	Explosion when added to rubber	T. R. Read	1976, 200, **57**, 592
Nitric oxide	Preparation	C. W. W. Read	1940, 83, **21**, 976
Nitric oxide	Carbon disulphide, burn with	C. W. W. Read	1940, 83, **21**, 977
Nitric oxide	Carbon disulphide, burns with blue flash	F. A Hatton	1963, 154, **44**, 701

Compound, Substance, Subject	Details, Reaction etc.	Author	Reference
p-Nitroacetanilide	Sulphuric acid conc. 'Pharaoh's Serpent's experiment; vigorous reaction at 200 °C, mild explosion	R. E. D. Clark	1934, 62, **16**, 271
Nitrobenzene	Poison	C. W. W. Read	1940, 83, **21**, 972
Nitrobenzene	Poison: inhalation and absorption consequences	D. R. Browning	1967, 166, **48**, 718
Nitrobenzene	Preparation	C. W. W. Read	1940, 83, **21**, 976
t-Nitrobutane	Distillation. Explosion	A. J. Mee	1940, 85, **22**, 95
Nitro compounds	Aromatic. Poisonous, absorbed by skin	S. I. Levy	1936, 68, **17**, 488
Nitro derivatives of benzene	Toxic, absorbed by skin in some cases	C. G. Vernon	1927, 34, **9**, 97
Nitro explosives	A brief survey of explosive systems I	S. I. Levy	1935, 67, **17**, 341
Nitro explosives	A brief survey of explosive systems II	S. I. Levy	1936, 68, **17**, 488
Nitrogen	Preparation	C. W. W. Read	1940, 83, **21**, 977
Nitrogen dioxide	Poison	C. W. W. Read	1940, 83, **21**, 973
Nitrogen dioxide	Preparation	C. W. W. Read	1940, 83, **21**, 976
Nitrogen oxides	Toxic: attack lungs	C. G. Vernon	1927, 34, **9**, 97
Nitrogen oxides	Higher. Poisonous	A. J. Mee	1940, 85, **22**, 95
Nitrogen tetroxide (dinitrogen tetraoxide)	Dissociation in sealed tube. Beware of putting cold tube in hot water (>45 °C), or explosion possible	L. Williams	1958, 138, **39**, 291
Nitrogen tetroxide	Dissociation of, poisonous nature of N_2O_4	T. A. H. Peacocke	1959, 141, **40**, 346
Nitrogen triiodide	Unstable detonator	S. I. Levy	1935, 67, **17**, 343
Nitrogen triiodide	Preparation	C. W. W. Read	1940, 83, **21**, 977
Nitroglycerine	Explosive	W. E. Garner	1933, 55, **14**, 250
Nitroglycerol (propane-1,2,3-triyl nitrate)	Preparation	C. W. W. Read	1940, 83, **21**, 977
Nitrophenols	Poison	C. W. W. Read	1940, 83, **21**, 972
Nitrous acid (nitric(III) acid)	Preparation: sucking back danger	—	1928, 38, **10**, 100
Nitrous fumes	Can cause severe poisoning	D. R. Browning	1968, 168, **49**, 606
Nitrous oxide (dinitrogen oxide)	Preparation	C. W. W. Read	1940, 83, **21**, 976
Nylon fishing line	Hazard if snaps under tension	—	*1978, 78, 22*
Oil	Hazard of converting to gas	—	*1972, 46, 22*
Organic preparations	Small-scale, safer reactions	J. H. Wilkinson	1955, 131, **37**, 91
Organic preparations	Small-scale, safer reactions	J. T. Stock, M. A. Fill	1961, 149, **43**, 130
Organo-lead compounds	Survey of hazards	A. K. Holliday W. Towers	1974, 195, **56**, 417
Organo-phosphorus compounds	Poisonous	R. S. Edmundson	1963, 155, **45**, 112
Osmic acid	Dangerous	A. R. A. Noel	1967, 165, **48**, 479
Overhead projector	Eye strain	G. L. Treglown	1968, 171, **50**, 434

Compound, Substance, Subject	Details, Reaction etc.	Author	Reference
Oxalic acid (ethanedioic acid)	Poison	C. W. W. Read	1940, 83, **21**, 973
Oxidation	Solids, by nitric acid	C. W. W. Read	1940, 83, **21**, 976
Oxides	Metallic, reduction by hydrogen dangerous	C. W. W. Read	1940, 83, **21**, 965, 968
Oxides	Reduction by hydrogen	C. W. W. Read	1940, 83, **21**, 976
Oxides	Reduction by coal gas	C. W. W. Read	1940, 83, **21**, 976
Oxides	Reduction. Method of avoiding danger with hydrogen	H. E. Watson	1943, 93, **24**, 211
Oxides, nitrogen	Higher oxides poisonous. *See* Nitrogen	A. J. Mee	1940, 85, **22**, 95
Oxygen	Preparation	C. W. W. Read	1940, 83, **21**, 976
Oxygen	Preparation: explosion when carbon involved instead of MnO_2	C. W. W. Read	1941, 87, **22**, 340
Oxygen	Preparation: Manganese dioxide, if pure, usable as catalyst	H. Tattersall	1956, 134, **38**, 132
Oxygen	Acetylene. Explosion	G. Fowles	1940, 85, **22**, 6
Oxygen	Acetylene. Explosion: extreme danger	C. Holt	1962, 152, **44**, 161
Oxygen	Acetylene. Violent explosion on ignition	P. D. Arculus	1963, 154, **44**, 706
Oxygen	Ammonia; oxidation reaction: pass ammonia over platinized asbestos. Beware vigorous reaction	D. Nealy	1935, 63, **16**, 410
Oxygen	Ammonia oxygen bubbled through	E. J. Williams	1935, 63, **16**, 410
Oxygen	Ammonia: Pt spiral catalyst—safe but violent	L. T. Taylor	1935, 63, **16**, 410
Oxygen	Ammonia: burn in	C. W. W. Read	1940, 83, **21**, 977
Oxygen	Coal gas blow pipe, warnings, explosion, fire, melted metals	G. W. Young	1948, 109, **29**, 368
Oxygen	Hydrocarbon explosions; precautions	T. A. H. Peacocke	1964, 156, **45**, 459
Oxygen	Hydrogen; explanation of why no explosion with hot silver wire	C. N. Hinshelwood	1927, 31, **8**, 171
Oxygen	Hydrogen: explosion with certain volumes in eudiometer: dangers	R. D. Reid	1928, 38, **10**, 149
Oxygen	Hydrogen. Form soap bubbles; harmless explosions	R. R. Finney	1935, 65, **17**, 137
Oxygen	Hydrogen, explosions: hazardous	C. W. W. Read	1940, 83, **21**, 976
Oxygen	Hydrogen, explosions	G. Fowles	1940, 85, **22**, 6
Oxygen	Hydrogen, explosions: extra care required	C. Holt	1962, 152, **44**, 161
Oxygen	Hydrogen, explosions: precautions	T. A. H. Peacocke	1964, 156, **45**, 459
Oxygen	Hydrogen, explosions: demonstration using polythene flask	J. W. Davis	1964, 157, **45**, 649
Oxygen	Hydrogen, explosions: demonstration using polythene bottle	E. V. Ogden	1964, 157, **45**, 674
Oxygen	Hydrogen, explosions: use balloon	B. Poole	1964, 158, **46**, 230

Compound, Substance, Subject	Details, Reaction etc.	Author	Reference
Oxygen	Hydrogen, explosions: safe experiment described	M. J. Clark	1965, 161, **47**, 177
Oxygen	Magnesium, burning in oxygen	C. W. W. Read	1940, 83, **21**, 968
Oxygen	Methane. Explosive reaction possible	T. G. Pearson	1940, 83, **21**, 923
Oxygen	Phosphorus burnt in	C. W. W. Read	1940, 83, **21**, 977
Oxygen	Sulphur burnt in	C. W. W. Read	1940, 83 **21**, 977
Oxygen	Advice on preparation	—	*1965, 14, 53–56*
Oxygen mixture	Hazards of	—	*1965, 14, 53–56,* and *1965, 13, 28–29*
Ozone (trioxygen)	Preparation	C. W. W. Read	1940, 83, **21**, 976
Ozonides	Decomposition of: ozonides highly explosive	G. N. Copley	1944, 97, **25**, 293
Peanut	Explosion in food calorimeter	I. Nuttall	1977, 205, **58**, 817
Pencil sharpener	Some contain magnesium and pose a hazard	—	*1975, 64, 16*
Pentyl nitrate	*See* Amyl nitrate		
Perchlorates	Dangerously explosive: details	A. J. Mee	1940, 85, **22**, 95
Perchloric acid	Preparation	C. W. W. Read	1940, 83, **21**, 977
Perchloric acid	Dangerously explosive: details	A. J. Mee	1940, 85, **22**, 95
Perchloric acid	Advice on storage, ordering and use	—	*1967, 21, 48*
Peroxides, dialphyl } Peroxides, diethyl }	Explosive	G. N. Copley	1939, 82, **21**, 871
Petrol vapour	Experimental 'safe' explosions: details for performing	W. Railston	1937, 74, **19**, 173
Petroleum	Suspected carcinogen	—	*1975, 64, 16*
Phenol	Blisters on skin	G. Fowles	1940, 85, **22**, 8
Phenol	Beware of on skin	T. C. Swinfen	1965, 160, **46**, 669
Phenol	Absorbed through skin can cause death	D. R. Browning	1967, 166 **48**, 918
Phenol	Conc. sulphuric acid, Phenol sulphonic acid formed: add nitric acid; violent reaction, nitrous fumes	S. I. Levy	1936, 68, **17**, 490
Phenol sulphonic acids	*See* Phenol		
Phenolic compounds	From fractional distillation of coal tar. Poisonous and corrosive	M. S. Parker	1965, 159, **46**, 345
Phenols	Poison	C. W. W. Read	1940, 83, **21**, 972
Phenylamine	*See* Aniline		
Phenylene diamines (benzene diamines)	Poisonous	C. W. W. Read	1940, 83, **21**, 972
Phenylhydrazine	Toxic	C. G. Vernon	1927, 34, **9**, 97
Phenylhydrazine	Poisonous	G. Fowles	1963, 153, **44**, 406
Phosgene (carbonyl chloride)	Highly toxic impurity sometimes present in chloroform	P. F. R. Venables	1942, 92, **24**, 26
Phosgene	Preparation	C. W. W. Read	1940, 83, **21**, 977
Phosgene, benzene	Benzophenone preparation. Relatively safe on small scale	J. T. Stock, M. A. Fill	1961, 149, **43**, 130

Compound, Substance, Subject	Details, Reaction etc.	Author	Reference
Phosgene, diphosgene	Lung irritants	F. F. Crossley	1940, 84, **21**, 1049
Phosphine		C. W. W. Read	1940, 83, **21**, 969
Phosphine	Toxic	C. G. Vernon	1927, 34, **9**, 97
Phosphine	Poison	E. A. Philpots	1933, 56, **14**, 489
Phosphine	Preparation	C. W. W. Read	1940, 83, **21**, 976
Phosphine	Preparation: 'safe' method	I. W. Williams	1968, 168, **49**, 487
Phosphorus	Yellow. Absorption effects. Ignites spontaneously	D. R. Browning	1967, 166, **48**, 718
Phosphorus	White. Burns	—	1928, 38, **10**, 97
Phosphorus	Burning; early reference	R. E. D. Clark	1933, 58, **15**, 143
Phosphorus	Yellow; don't handle	C. W. W. Read	1940, 83, **21**, 973, 4
Phosphorus	Burning dangers	E. H. Coulson, L. F. Ennever	1942, 90, **23**, 230
Phosphorus	Explosion possible	E. A. Philpots	1933, 56, **14**, 489
Phosphorus	Inflammable, dangerously spontaneous under warm, humid conditions	A. W. S. Watson	1966, 164, **48**, 267
Phosphorus	White, toxic	C. G. Vernon	1927, 34, **9**, 97
Phosphorus	Bromine, water. Danger of explosion	A. J. Mee	1940, 85, **22**, 95
Phosphorus	Carbon disulphide, solution in	C. W. W. Read	1940, 83, **21**, 976
Phosphorus	Chlorate: mixture explosive	H. K. Black	1963, 153, **44**, 462
Phosphorus	Ethyl bromide preparation	C. W. W. Read	1940, 83, **21**, 976
Phosphorus	Iodine, alcohol. Ethyl iodide preparation dangerous	C. W. W. Read	1940, 83, **21**, 967
Phosphorus	Metals, handling and disposal of phosphorus hazardous	P. D. Arculus	1958, 140, **40**, 151
Phosphorus	Oxygen, burn in	C. W. W. Read	1940, 83, **21**, 977
Phosphorus	Red; potassium chlorate. Explosive even without heat	—	1923, 18, **5**, 112
Phosphorus	Red; potassium chlorate. Explosive	—	1928, 38, **10**, 97
Phosphorus	Yellow; sodium hydroxide. 'Safe' method for phosphine details	I. W. Williams	1968, 168, **49**, 487
Phosphorus, red	Fire with plastic sinks	A. B. Newall	*1972, 47, 24*
Phosphorus, white	Fire in outside brick store	R. J. Mitchell	*1979, 82, 29*
Phosphorus chlorides	Avoid preparation	C. W. W. Read	1940, 83, **21**, 976
Phosphorus, organic compounds of	Poisonous	J. C. Curry	1965, 160, **46**, 770
Phosphorus trichloride	Possible fires etc.	—	1928, 38, **10**, 100
Phosphorus trichloride	Preparation	R. J. Kerr Muir	1940, 83, **21**, 1007
Phosphorus trichloride	Glacial acetic acid. Acetyl chloride preparation. Report of explosion	T. A. H. Peacocke	1962, 152, **44**, 217
Phosphorus tri- and pen-tachloride	Preparation	C. W. W. Read	1940, 83, **21**, 969
Phthalic anhydride (benzene-1,2-dicarboxylic anhydride)	Anhydrous copper oxide. Explosive when heated	A. J. Mee	1940, 85, **22**, 95
Picric acid (2,4,6-trinitrophenol)	Poison	C. W. W. Read	1940, 83, **21**, 972

Compound, Substance, Subject	Details, Reaction etc.	Author	Reference
Pipettes, mouth	Hazards of use	F. C. Brown	1971, 181, **52**, 990
Pipetting alkalis	Safe only for sixth formers	C. W. W. Read	1940, 83, **21**, 977
Pitch	Constituent of; producer of cancer	C. Doreé	1937, 72, **18**, 498
Plastic syringes, disposable	Not to be obtained from hospitals	—	*1976, 67, 15* and *1976, 201, 57, 784*
Plutonium	Remote control handling. Critical mass	J. M. Thomas	1959, 143, **41**, 33
Plutonium 239	D.E.S. advice to withdraw sources	—	*1974, 58, 22*
Plutonium chemistry	Fitted glove box needed when handling	F. R. Paulsen	1955, 131, **37**, 49
Poisons	Solid and gas	—	1929, 41, **11**, 22, 23
Poisons	Storage of	E. A. Philpots	1933, 56, **14**, 489
Poisons	Note on Scheduled Poisons	C. W. W. Read	1940, 83, **21**, 971
Poisons	'Their Properties, Chemical Identification, Symptoms and Emergency. Treatment'. Review	V. J. Brookes, H. N. Alyea	1948, 110, **30**, 132
Polonium	Body tolerance 10^{-12} g	T. A. H. Peacocke	1954, 127, **35**, 355
P.T.F.E. (polytetrafluoroethene)	Toxic fumes above 350 °C	—	1958, 140, **40**, 208
P.T.F.E.	Toxic fumes (highly) on heating	J. L. Latham, W. F. Tyler	1961, 149, **43**, 151
Polypropylene sinks	*See* Sinks		
Polystyrene sinks	*See* Sinks		
Polyurethanes	*See* Di-isocyanates		
Potassium	To be used only by teachers	C. W. W. Read	1940, 83, **21**, 976
Potassium	Do not handle, avoid contact with water	C. W. W. Read	1940, 83, **21**, 973, 974
Potassium	Explosion on cutting: metal was stored in naphtha	D. P. Pomeroy	1946, 103, **27**, 422
Potassium	Preparation by Brunner's method (K_2CO_3+C): product contains explosive potassium carbonyl	J. G. F. Druce	1926, 28, **7**, 261
Potassium	Hydrogen equivalent, measurement of. Danger of explosion	D. M. T. Casey	1964, 156, **45**, 411
Potassium	Water. Explosion danger; minimization	W. W. Allen	1937, 72, **18**, 600
Potassium	Water	C. W. W. Read	1941, 87, **22**, 340
Potassium	Water. Explosion when restricted	L. H. Angus	1950, 115, **31**, 402
Potassium	Water. Safer method of collecting hydrogen, using liquid paraffin	K. I. P. Adamson	1964, 158, **46**, 178
Potassium acetate (ethanoate)	Lead nitrate. Explosion when heated	A. J. Mee	1940, 85, **22**, 95
Potassium antimonyl tartrate	Effect of swallowing	—	1928, 38, **10**, 102
Potassium carbonate	Magnesium. Explosive substance formed	J. G. F. Druce	1926, 28, **7**, 261

Compound, Substance, Subject	Details, Reaction etc.	Author	Reference
Potassium carbonate	Magnesium. Castellana fusion: possible explosion	G. Fowles	1938, 77, **20**, 124
Potassium chlorate	Preparation	C. W. W. Read	1940, 83, **21**, 977
Potassium chlorate	Heat. Possible explosion	—	1928, 38, **10**, 99
Potassium chlorate	Heat	C. W. W. Read	1940, 83, **21**, 976
Potassium chlorate	Manganese dioxide. Possible explosion on heating	—	1928, 38, **10**, 99
Potassium chlorate	Phosphorus, red. Explosion, even without heat	—	1923, 18, **5**, 112
Potassium chlorate	Phosphorus, red	—	1928, 38, **10**, 97
Potassium chlorate	Sugar, conc. sulphuric acid. Explosive precautions	—	1923, 18, **5**, 112
Potassium chlorate	Sulphur. Explosion	C. W. W. Read	1940, 83, **21**, 969
Potassium chlorate	Sulphur	C. W. W. Read	1940, 83, **21**, 976
Potassium chlorate	Sulphuric acid	C. W. W. Read	1940, 83, **21**, 976
Potassium cyanide	Teachers only should use it	C. W. W. Read	1940, 83, **21**, 976
Potassium cyanide	Antidote for	E. J. Williams	1937, 74, **19**, 308
Potassium cyanide	Poison, deadly. Technique to avoid in analysis	R. Chandra	1962, 150, **43**, 451
Potassium cyanide	Further notes on avoidance in analysis	G. Fowles	1963, 153, **44**, 406
Potassium dichromate dust	Suspected carcinogenic	D. R. Browning	1967, 167, **49**, 278
Potassium hydroxide		C. W. W. Read	1940, 83, **21**, 972
Potassium hydroxide	Caution when solution used in syringe	—	1976, 69, 29
Potassium nitrate	Sulphur, charcoal, explosion when ground	—	1923, 18, **5**, 112
Potassium permanganate	Hydrochloric acid drops. Explosion reported	J. C. Curry	1965, 160, **46**, 770
Potassium permanganate	Sulphuric acid conc. Explosion when warmed	L. R. Wheeler	1929, 39, **10**, 274
Potassium permanganate	Sulphuric acid conc. Manganese heptoxide explodes violently on warming	—	1930, 46, **12**, 178
Propane-1,2,3-triol	See Glycerol		
Propane-1,2,3-triyl nitrate	See Nitroglycerol		
Propanone	Explosion on mixing with trichloromethane	E. H. Coulson	1974, 192, **55**, 596
Propanone	Explosive mixture with chloroform	—	1974, 57, 38
Propenoates	See Acrylic esters		
Prop-2-en-1-ol	See Allyl alcohol		
Proscribed chemicals	Difficulty of producing a satisfactory list	—	1978, 78, 22–23
Protoactinium	Uranium cow experiment. Contamination avoided by means of tray	T. A. H. Peacocke	1962, 152, **44**, 137
Prussic acid (hydrogen cyanide)	Preparation. (See also Cyanides)	C. W. W. Read	1940, 83, **21**, 977

Compound, Substance, Subject	Details, Reaction etc.	Author	Reference
Pyridine	Danger to eyes, heart. Details	D. R. Browning	1967, 166, **48**, 718
Pyrotechnics	Case for and against	—	*1963, 5, 53–54*
Radiation	Precautions with radioactive materials	R. M. Fishenden	1949, 112, **30**, 306 1949, 112, **30**, 311 1949, 112, **30**, 314
Radiation	Dangers; effect on man	F. W. Spiers	1958, 139, **39**, 450
Radiation	Hazard, details	Min. of Ed.	1959, 141, **40**, 363
Radiation	'Radiation. Dangers and what they mean to you': review of book	H. W. Heckstall-Smith	1959, 141, **40**, 394
Radiation	Effects of	P. A. Barker	1959, 143 **41**, 169
Radiation	Biological effects of	P. J. Lindop	1961, 147, **42**, 223
Radiation	'Radiation, Genes and Man': review of book	B. Wallace, T Dobzhansky	1961, 149, **43**, 235
Radiation	'Radiation, Hazards and Protection': review of book	D. E. Barnes, D. Taylor	1963, 155, **45**, 274
Radioactive isotopes	Hazards and precautions	U.K.A.E.A.	1958, 140, **40**, 179
Radioactive materials	Safe transport of: film review	U.K.A.E.A.	1966, 162, **47**, 582
Radioactive sources	Precautions: Ra^{226}, Co^{60}, Sr^{90} etc.	J. W. Lucas	1966, 164, **48**, 19
Radioactive substances	Report of A.S.E. sub-committee	—	1959, 143, **41**, 173
Radioactive tablet scheme	Details of sources and how to obtain them	U.K.A.E.A.	1967, 165, **48**, 571
Radioactivity experiments	Precautions	K. Forster	1965, 159, **46**, 397
Radiochemistry	Some experiments for schools	T. A. H. Peacocke	1954, 127, **35**, 354
Radiochemistry	Suggested experiments for schools	N. H. Davies	1965, 161, **47**, 152
Radiochemistry	Experiments, precautions, disposal	T. A. H. Peacocke	1964, 157, **45**, 597
Radiochemistry	Solution, chemical systems in: generally not safe to handle in lecture theatre	P. A. Murfin	1957, 137, **39**, 39 1957, 137, **39**, 41
Radiochemistry, practical	Review of book: stresses health precautions	M. F. C. Ladd, W. H. Lee	1964, 158, **46**, 257
Radio-isotopes	'The measurement of Radio-isotopes': review. Chapter on health hazards	D. Taylor	1952, 120, **33**, 283
Radon	Radiation danger	C. G. Ferguson	1946, 102, **27**, 179
Ragwort	*See Senecio* spp.		
Resorcinol	Formaldehyde resin: explosion	—	*1971, 45, 36*
Rocksill	Hazards of oxidizable impurities	—	*1976, 70, 29*
Rocksill wool	Explosions with manganate(VII)	B. J. Hallam, M. Armstrong	1975, 197, **56**, 82
Safeguards in School Laboratories	Comments on L.E.A. Regulations	G. Fowles	1940, 85, **22**, 3
Safety	Carcinoma-inducing compounds	D. R. Browning	1967, 167, **49**, 278
Safety	The teacher's duty	D. R. Browning	1967, 166, **48**, 918

Compound, Substance, Subject	Details, Reaction etc.	Author	Reference
Safety	Accidents with Tollen's reagent	D. R. Browning	1968, 168, **49,** 605
Safety	D.E.S. advice	—	1976, 69, 20–21, 1976, 68, 9 and 1978, 79, 22–23
Safety	Check list	—	1977, 75, 18–19
Safety	Need for positive advice	B. D. Sorsby	1978, 77, 22
Safety	And professional judgement	L. J. Campbell	1977, 71, 22 (and 1976, 68, 20–21)
Safety equipment	Responsibility for providing	—	1976, 67, 14
Safety in the Chemical Laboratory	Book by H. A. J. Pieters and J. W. Creyghton	Review	1951, 118 **32,** 411
Safety in the Laboratory	Book by J. N. Friend	Review	1958, 140, **40,** 233
Safety in School Chemistry	How do textbooks deal with hazards?	D. R. Browning	1967, 166, **48,** 717
Safety Precautions in Schools	M. of Ed. Pamphlet	Review	1961, 148, **42,** 582
Safety spectacles	*See* Eye protection		
Sealing tube ends	Accidental	—	1928, 38, **10,** 101
Selenium compounds	Biological methylation of	F. Challenger	1936, 68, **17,** 575
Senecio spp.	Toxic and carcinogenic alkaloids of these spp.	J. R. Martin	1975, 199, **57,** 391
Silica	Magnesium. Detonation if silica not completely dry	W. B. Barker	1938, 77, **20,** 150
Silicate	Sodium hydroxide: fused bead. When hot, explosion may take place when bead dipped into water	P. Heath	1956, 132, **37,** 250
Silicon(IV) chloride	Explosion of stock bottle	—	1971, 41, 34
Silicon(IV) chloride	Explosion	J. A. Kirk	1969, 34, 49
Silicon(IV) chloride	Explosion (by hydrolysis?)	A. J. Maclean	1969, 35, 38
Silicon(IV) chloride	Bursting of bottle	—	1970, 37, 42–43
Silicon tetrachloride	*See* Silicon(IV) chloride		
Silicon tetrachloride	Storage and handling advice	—	1979, 85, 31
Silver acetylide (silver(I) dicarbide)	Unstable detonator	S. I. Levy	1935, 67, **17,** 343
Silver ions	Ammonium ions. Substance heated to expel ammonia; Devarda's alloy added: violent explosion	J. Baldwin	1967, 165, **48,** 586
Silver nitrate	Powder, magnesium powder. Explodes immediately on adding drop of cold water	D. J. Lyness, K. Hutton	1953, 125, **35,** 138
Silver oxalate	Heat: likely to explode	W. E. Garner	1933, 55, **14,** 247
Silver oxide ppt.	Ammonia. When hot, explosion. Fulminate possibly formed	J. R. Morse	1955, 131, **37,** 147
Silver oxide ppt.	Ammoniacal, caustic soda. Explosion on standing	E. Green	1965, 161, **47,** 231
Silver oxide ppt.	Ammonia, dissolved in; ppted. by $AgNO_3$. Solution exploded on standing	D. R. Browning	1968, 168, **49,** 605

Compound, Substance, Subject	Details, Reaction etc.	Author	Reference
Sinks	Fire with phosphorus	A. B. Newall	*1972, 47, 24*
Sinks, polypropylene	Hazards of	—	*1971, 43, 24* and *1971, 45, 35*
Sinks, polystyrene	Hazards of	—	*1971, 43, 24*
Soda	Molten, dry chlorine	J. Bradley	1968, 168, **49**, 454
Sodium	Metal	C. W. W. Read	1940, 83, **21**, 976
Sodium	Wire	May & Baker	1956, 133, **37**, 446
Sodium	Burns	—	1928, 38, **10**, 97
Sodium	Explosion possible	E. A. Philpots	1933, 56, **14**, 489
Sodium	Do not handle, or allow in contact with water	C. W. W. Read	1940, 83, **21**, 973, 974
Sodium	Handling dangers	J. Allsop	1949, 113, **31**, 133
Sodium	Preparation. Davy's isolation of, from caustic soda. Spitting. Screen	E. R. Martin	1925, 25, **7**, 39
Sodium	Hydrogen equivalent measurement of. Explosion danger	M. T. Casey	1964, 156, **45**, 411
Sodium	Lassaigne's test. Some compounds explode when heated with sodium in organic analysis	G. Fowles	1938, 77, **20**, 124
Sodium	Water. Violent explosion	—	1922, 14, **4**, 97
Sodium	Water. Possible explanation and avoidance of explosion	—	1922, 16, **4**, 216
Sodium	Water. Reason for possible explosion; precautions	J. A. Cochrane	1928, 35, **9**, 234
Sodium	Water. Explosion possible, particularly in confined space	—	1928, 38, **10**, 100
Sodium	Water. Explosion with	C. Baily	1935, 65, **17**, 146
Sodium	Water. Explosion danger; minimization	W. W. Allen	1937, 72, **18**, 600
Sodium	Water. Teacher demonstration	C. W. W. Read	1940, 83, **21**, 976
Sodium	Water. A method of minimizing danger using metal apparatus	M. T. Casey	1957, 136, **38**, 424
Sodium	Use of metal	—	1970, 176, **51**, 707
Sodium	Water. Explosion risk; further comment	L. H. Angus	1958, 138, **39**, 321
Sodium	Water. Safer method of collecting hydrogen	K. I. P. Adamson	1964, 158, **46**, 178
Sodium	Water. Method of performing demonstration	C. Holt	1966, 164, **48**, 171
Sodium	Water. A class experiment with care	J. P. C. Watson	1967, 166, **48**, 924
Sodium	Violent reaction with a detergent solution	M. A. Shaw	*1979, 82, 33*
Sodium azide	Nitrogen source. Detonates on rapid heating. Demonstration	B. Lambert	1927, 31, **8**, 218
Sodium chlorate(I)	*See* sodium hypochlorite		
Sodium fluoride	Poison	C. W. W. Read	1940, 83, **21**, 972
Sodium fusions	Performed by teacher only	C. W. W. Read	1940, 83, **21**, 976
Sodium fusions	Middleton's procedure is safer	G. Fowles	1940, 85, **22**, 6

Compound, Substance, Subject	Details, Reaction etc.	Author	Reference
Sodium hydroxide	Poison	C. W. W. Read	1940, 83, **21,** 972
Sodium hydroxide	Skin, dangers to	T. C. Swinfen	1965, 160, **46,** 670
Sodium hydroxide	Ammonium compound, boiling with	C. W. W. Read	1940, 83, **21,** 968
Sodium hypochlorite	Explosion of bottle	—	*1971, 43, 24*
Sodium nitrate	Sodium thiosulphate. Mixture exploded when heated	—	1947, 107, **28,** 386
Sodium nitrate	Sodium thiosulphate. Mixture exploded when heated	A. J. Mee	1940, 85, **22,** 95
Sodium nitrate(III)	Toxicity	G. C. Britton	1975, 198, **57,** 186
Sodium peroxide	Substance blown out of bottle on releasing stopper	N. F. Watterson	1935, 64, **16,** 569
Sodium peroxide	Explosion: possible explanation	C. Baily	1935, 65, **17,** 146
Sodium peroxide	Explosion: explanation; air and organic substances react causing ignition	F. L. Swift	1935, 66, **17,** 310
Sodium peroxide	Dangerous	G. Fowles	1955, 130, **36,** 417
Sodium peroxide	Hydrogen sulphide ignited by trace of Na_2O_2	A. J. Mee	1940, 85, **22,** 95
Sodium peroxide	Water. Oxygen preparation. Beware excess sodium present: explosive hydrogen-oxygen mixture likely	W. B. Barker	1935, 63, **16,** 438
Sodium peroxide	Water: denial of explosion	A. Adair	1935, 67, **17,** 439
Sodium silicofluoride	Poison	C. W. W. Read	1940, 83, **21,** 972
Sodium thiosulphate	Sodium nitrate. Mixture exploded when heated	—	1947, 106, **28,** 386
Sodium thiosulphate	Sodium nitrate. Exploded when heated	A. J. Mee	1940, 85, **22,** 3
Solids	Decomposition and detonation of	W. E. Garner	1933, 55, **14,** 244–51
Soxhlet extractions	Undesirable in schools	C. W. W. Read	1940, 83, **21,** 977
Spirit burners	Fire hazards	—	*1979, 85, 30–31*
Storage	Safety hazards if inadequate	—	*1970, 37, 47*
Sugar	Chlorate mixture: explosive	H. K. Black	1963, 153, **44,** 462
Sugar	Potassium chlorate, sulphuric acid conc. Explosive: precautions	—	1923, 18, **5,** 112
Sulphamic acid (aminosulphonic acid)	Skin, precautions with	J. G. Stark	1965, 161, **47,** 171
Sulphonal	Poison	C. W. W. Read	1940, 83, **21,** 972
Sulphur	Aluminium	C. W. W. Read	1940, 83, **21,** 977
Sulphur	Carbon disulphide, solution in	C. W. W. Read	1940, 83, **21,** 976
Sulphur	Charcoal, potassium nitrate. Grind: explosive	—	1923, 18, **5,** 112
Sulphur	Chlorate mixture: liable to spontaneous ignition, detonation	H. K. Black	1963, 153, **44,** 463
Sulphur	Magnesium	C. W. W. Read	1940, 83, **21,** 977
Sulphur	Magnesium. Heat: explosion	K. Hutton	1950, 114, **31,** 265
Sulphur	Oxygen, burn in	C. W. W. Read	1940, 83, **21,** 976

Compound, Substance, Subject	Details, Reaction etc.	Author	Reference
Sulphur	Potassium chlorate. Explosion	C. W. W. Read	1940, 83, **21**, 969
Sulphur	Potassium	C. W. W. Read	1940, 83, **21**, 976
Sulphur	Zinc	C. W. W. Read	1940, 83, **21**, 976
Sulphur chlorides	Preparation	C. W. W. Read	1940, 83, **21**, 977
Sulphur dioxide	Poison	—	1929, 41, **11**, 22
Sulphur dioxide	Poisonous, corrosive; disadvantages as refrigerant	V. A. Carpenter	1952, 120, **33**, 173
Sulphur dioxide	Preparation	C. W. W. Read	1940, 83, **21**, 976
Sulphur dioxide	Explosion danger in criticial temp. expt.	B. J. Bedell	1938, 77, **20**, 148
Sulphur trioxide	Water. Violent reaction	E. S. Dewing	1955, 131, **37**, 27
Sulphuric acid	Conc. Burns. Antidote	H. Garnett	1929, 40, **10**, 350
Sulphuric acid	Poison	C. W. W. Read	1940, 83, **21**, 972
Sulphuric acid	Preparation. Chamber, contact processes	C. W. W. Read	1940, 83, **21**, 969
Sulphuric acid	Preparation. Chamber process model	C. W. W. Read	1940, 83, **21**, 976
Sulphuric acid	Preparation. Contact process demonstration	C. W. W. Read	1940, 83, **21**, 977
Sulphuric acid	Collection of gases over: dangerous	—	1963, 154, **44**, 740
Sulphuric acid	Conc. Use in Dreschel bottles	C. W. W. Read	1940, 83, **21**, 977
Sulphuric acid	Conc. Desiccant in chlorine prepn.: suck back danger	A. Adair	1962, 152, **44**, 159
Sulphuric acid	Conc. Expansion of gas measurement with: dangerous	E. B. Rodmell	1961, 149, 343, 199
Sulphuric acid	Conc. Copper. Caution when adding Cu to hot acid: violent reaction	G. Fowles	1927, 34, **9**, 90
Sulphuric acid	Copper. Preparation of SO_2 dangerous	D. A. Campbell	1939, 80, **20**, 631
Sulphuric acid	Copper. Preparation of SO_2 dangerous	C. W. W. Read	1940, 83, **21**, 969
Sulphuric acid	Heat to decompose	C. W. W. Read	1940, 83, **21**, 977
Sulphuric acid	Iron filings. $FeSO_4$ preparation	C. W. W. Read	1940, 83, **21**, 969
Sulphuric acid	Potassium chlorate	C. W. W. Read	1940, 83, **21**, 976
Sulphuric acid	Treatment of burns	J. T. Burton	*1976, 67, 16*
Syringes disposable	Potential hazard	A. Farmer	1971, 182, **53**, 231
Syringes disposable	*See* Plastic syringes		
Tetrachloromethane	*See* Carbon tetrachloride		
Thallium	Poison	C. W. W. Read	1940, 83, **21**, 972
Thallium	Element and compounds too toxic for schools	A. W. Bamford	1976, 201, **57**, 784
Thermit process	Fusing: safe method / Fusing: dangerous methods	E. Walker / A. D. Macdonald	1956, 133, **37**, 435
Thermit process	Magnesium, sodium peroxide; potassium chlorate, sulphur	O. J. Elphick	1957, 135, **38**, 295
Thermit process	Fusing. Aluminium, iodine fuse recommended	C. M. Hammerton	1957, 136, **38**, 459

Compound, Substance, Subject	Details, Reaction etc.	Author	Reference
Thermit process	Ignition, further comment	C. Chittock	1958, 138, **39**, 323
Thermit process	Ignition, further comment: sodium peroxide, magnesium ignition possibly dangerous	L. H. Angus	1958, 140, **40**, 154
Thermit process	Ignition: match heads safe	E. C. Weaver	1959, 142, **40**, 555
Thermit process	Fuse, discussion: possible danger of chlorate mixtures	Editors of *Science Masters' Book IV*, 2	1966, 162, **47**, 560
Thermit process	Fuse	N. Le Poidevin	1966, 164, **48**, 243
Thermit process	Explosion with copper oxide	T. E. W. Browne	1967, 166, **48**, 921
Thioacetamide	Skin: may be harmful if absorbed through	B. E. Dawson	1961, 147, **42**, 220
Thiocyanates	Danger of HCN when oxidized	G. J. Cooper	*1967, 24, 33*
Thorium	Uranium cow experiment. Avoid contamination by means of tray	T. A. H. Peacocke	1962, 152, **44**, 137
Thorium hydroxide	Salt preparation from. Fume cupboard, gloves	T. A. H. Peacocke	1954, 127, **35**, 356
Tin(IV) chloride	Preparation to be avoided?	C. W. W. Read	1940, 83, **21**, 969
Tollen's reagents	Exploded after leaving	E. Green	1965, 161, **48**, 231
Tollen's reagent	Exploded while being prepared	D. R. Browning	1967, 166, **48**, 920
Tollen's reagent	Explosions recorded	D. R. Browning	1968, 168, **49**, 605
Toluene (methylbenzene) and some homologues	Toxic	C. G. Vernon	1927, 34, **9**, 97
Toxic agents	'Laboratory Handbook of Toxic Reagents' (C. H. Gray)	Reviews of this book	1961, 148, **42**, 581 1967, 165, **48**, 614
Toxic chemicals	Inorganic and organic	C. G. Vernon	1927, 34, **9**, 97
Trichloromethane	*See* Chloroform		
Trifluoroacetic acid (trifluoroethanoic acid)	Vesicant	J. Ormston	1945, 99, **26**, 151
Trinitrotoluene	Explodes with detonator	S. I. Levy	1935, 67, **17**, 343
Trinitrotoluene	Vapour volatile in steam: poisonous	S. I. Levy	1936, 68, **17**, 495
Tripods	Dangers when hot; storage	C. Holt	1968, 168, **49**, 492
Turpentine	Inflammable	C. W. W. Read	1940, 83, **21**, 973
Ultra-violet light	Absorption: glass containing 5% nickel oxide absorbs U.V. light, produces fluorescence	W. J. R. Calvert	1921, 7, **2**, 258
Ultra-violet light	Goggles needed to work with	F. H. Pollard *et al.*	1952, 122, **34**, 34
Water	Composition of, by volume. Dangers of amyl alcohol vapour surrounding eudiometer tube (inflammable vapour)	W. B. Barker	1935, 63, **16**, 415
Water	Composition of, by volume. 'Safe method'	W. V. Lloyd, F. J. Knight	1940, 84, **21**, 1144

Compound, Substance, Subject	Details, Reaction etc.	Author	Reference
Wet asbestos technique	Avoid	D. H. Mansfield	*1967, 25, 26*
X-rays	Apparatus dangers. Radiation. High potential	F. Mason	1938, 76, **19**, 532
X-rays	Hazards from 'Maltese cross' experiment	—	1959, 143, **41**, 173
Xylyl bromide	Lachrymator	F. F. Crossley	1940, 84, **21**, 1049
Ziegler process	Polyethylene preparation. Precautions with spontaneously inflammable aluminium triethyl, also highly toxic	T. A. H. Peacocke	1962, 150, **43**, 453
Zinc	Dust. Explosion risk	S. Robson	1934, 62, **16**, 165
Zinc	Sulphur	C. W. W. Read	1940, 83, **21**, 976

Index

Items listed in Appendix B are not included in the following index unless they are also referred to in the text.